Drink in the Wild

Drink in the Wild

Teas, Cordials, Jams and More

By HILARY STEWART

With drawings and photographs by the author

Douglas & McIntyre

VANCOUVER / TORONTO

Revised edition of the book originally published under
the title *Wild Teas, Coffees & Cordials*

Douglas & McIntyre
2323 Quebec Street, Suite 201
Vancouver, British Columbia
V5T 4S7

National Library of Canada Cataloguing in Publication Data

Stewart, Hilary, 1924–
Drink in the wild
Previous ed. has title: Wild teas, coffees & cordials.
Includes bibliographical references.
ISBN 1-55054-894-8
1. Wild plants, Edible—Northwest, Pacific. 2. Herbal teas.
3. Coffee substitutes—Northwest, Pacific. 4. Liqueurs—
Northwest, Pacific. 5. Jam—Northwest, Pacific. I. Stewart,
Hilary, 1924– Wild teas, coffees & cordials.
II. Title.
QK98.5.U6S84 2002   581.6'32'09795   C2001-911637-3

Cover design by Sigrid Albert
Cover photograph © Yogi, Inc./CORBIS/MAGMA
Text design by Robert Bringhurst
Printed and bound in Canada by Friesens
Printed on acid-free paper

We gratefully acknowledge the financial support of the
Canada Council for the Arts, the British Columbia Ministry
of Tourism, Small Business and Culture, and the
Government of Canada through the Book Publishing Industry
Development Program (BPIDP) for our publishing activities.

Acknowledgements

This book has been put together with many kinds of help, some of it given over many years. Much of the help has come as solid advice and factual information, some in less tangible ways.

To the following people I extend my very warm thanks and appreciation:

Ted Braidner, instructor of the first survival course I took, a man of infinite experience in outdoor skills, who introduced me to the astounding possibilities of food and drink from the wilds; Jim Boulding, cornerstone of Strathcona Park Lodge Outdoor Centre on Vancouver Island, who steered me through the rig-ours of my second survival course when genuine hunger made wild foraging a necessity and a practical way of learning, and who, in subsequent years, gave me the opportunity to experi-ence the wilderness beaches of the Island's west coast, where the idea for this book was born; George Clutesi, well-known Indian author and storyteller from the west coast of Vancouver Island, whose wise words have guided my attitude to all living and growing things; and Nancy Turner, ethnobotanist with the British Columbia Provincial Museum, and author of several books on plant uses, who has over the years answered my queries, encouraged my work on this book and generously shared some of her storehouse of knowledge with me.

I wish to extend special thanks to John Pinder-Moss of the University of British Columbia's herbarium, who patiently found the answers to my lists of questions, and who diligently went through the completed manuscript and drawings, corrected my errors and omissions and made worthwhile suggestions.

Contents

Quod in libro continetur

Fireweed gone to seed near the beach at Yuquot,
on the west coast of Vancouver Island

Introduction

LIMPETS WITH CHOPPED WILD ONIONS SAUTEED IN BUTTER for an appetizer. Succulent fresh salmon roasted over an open fire with a dish of wild beach peas and another of green goosefoot for the main course. Huckleberries mixed with salal berries for dessert. All this followed by a choice of richly aromatic spruce tea, or coffee from the roasted seeds of northern bedstraw.

Such was the evening meal, some years ago, for about a dozen assorted people on a remote beach on the west coast of Vancouver Island, British Columbia. They were taking a week's course learning how to survive in the wilderness and were using all aspects of the coastal environment to provide themselves with shelter, warmth, food and drink. The meal had been both satisfying and nutritious; they had enjoyed catching and cleaning the salmon, identifying and gathering the berries and potherbs, preparing the food, and they had discovered several textures and flavours new to them. A young man wondered aloud why more people didn't eat from the wilderness larder, and a woman remarked that, apart from the salmon, the best part of the meal had been the tea. She said there were many books available on wild edibles, but none specifically devoted to drinks.

And so the idea for this book was born—on a wide crescent of sandy beach with cresting waves smashing against the offshore island. A circling eagle eyed the salmon head left for it on the reef rock as I poured myself another mug of the fragrant spruce tea. As the person responsible for teaching wild edible foraging to the survival group, I could appreciate the need for a comprehensive guide book to the different drinks available from the wilds. I began collecting information on more teas and coffees, and other drinks too, keeping it all together in a folder labelled *wild drinks*—much to the amusement of those who noticed the file on my cluttered desk. I gathered leaves, flowers and seeds, steeped, boiled, brewed and roasted them and experimented in mixing the different flavours. My kitchen cupboards filled up with jars of funny-looking green stuff and I soon learned that careful labelling was essential. Whole leaves shrivelled out of recognition, and a jar with a Ginger Marmalade label was no help. I decided to focus on teas and other drinks of the Pacific Northwest which could be enjoyed for their own sake and to avoid those made for medicinal purposes only. There are already several good books on herbal medicines, and writing a book on that subject carries greater responsibility than I was willing to undertake. Books exist too on making coffee from grains, so I have not included wild grains in this one.

In addition to many herbal teas and a few coffees, I soon learned that the wilds—and sometimes even my own back garden—offered the ingredients for a variety of other drinks: cool lemonades, hot spicy concoctions, refreshing juices and even cordials. These I have included. Each season that passed afforded me the opportunity to try different tasting drinks, and each year I added a few new ingredients to the cupboard.

I have kept the contents of this book as simple as possible so that those without much knowledge of botany can still find and identify the plants and make the drinks. The ones I have in-cluded are not ordered according to family, as they would be in a work for scholars, and botanical terms requiring explanation have been omitted.

Plants are listed alphabetically by their most common names. Each is followed by its botanical name, with other names listed below. Some of the plants will already be familiar to you—at least by sight; others requiring some specialized habitat may not. Although the fifty plants of this book are all found in the Pacific Northwest, a great many of them also grow right across Canada and the United States.

The detailed instructions and the notes beside them should confirm the identification of the plant. Check these carefully, and if you are at all unsure, consult an authority—either a reputable botanical guidebook or a knowledgeable person—before using any part of the plant for a drink. WARNING: *never eat or drink anything from the wilds unless you can positively identify it, and know for certain that it is harmless.*

Measurements of plants and their various parts are given first in the metric system, followed by the rough equivalent in inches or feet, shown in brackets. Since leaf and flower sizes are not constant, an exact conversion is not necessary. Approximate measurements are also used in the instructions for preparation of the drinks. To accommodate the hiker or backpacker carrying a minimum of equipment, measurements such as "a generous handful," "a cup" or "a heaping teaspoonful" are used in preference to precise quantities. It matters not how large the hand, the cup or the teaspoon (even a wild guess will do), since the strength of a flavour often needs to be personally adjusted; the given measurement is not an instruction but a guide.

I would like the reader not to look upon these drinks as substitutes for "the real thing." Each has its own distinctive flavour; each is a drink in its own right and is not second best to any other drink, although you will undoubtedly prefer some to others.

Some plants, such as strawberry, clover, mint and pine, have several different species. Generally, they all make reasonable drinks when prepared in the same way as the plant shown; try them and see which you prefer.

Early explorers, settlers and miners drank a variety of teas from the bush to eke out precious supplies of imported teas, or used them when the tea caddy was empty and the ship bringing new supplies had not arrived. But often the wild teas were the only kinds they had, and these they enjoyed for their fragrance and aromatic flavours. So be adventurous. Explore the possibilities of these drinks. Don't expect supermarket flavours, but do be prepared to discover new and different tastes. The benefits are many: walking in the outdoors, whatever the season, can take on an added interest and provide a sense of discovery and accomplishment which you can share with others. Besides, the drinks made from these plants contain no additives, preservatives or caffeine—and no price tag.

For this revised edition, I have added recipes for jams and jellies and some other uses (along with new drawings) for the plants. Some of the recipes were given to me by friends, though others have lost their originators. To all who have added to my old ragged notebook of "What You Can Do with Wild Stuff," my warm thanks.

Above, wild blackberries in the city; below, clover
among the uncut grass on a side street

Harvesting the Plants

Where to Harvest

Wild plants suitable for making natural drinks can be found growing anywhere from cracks in city sidewalks to the most remote mountain wilderness. City and urban dwellers will find a good choice by scouting vacant lots and undeveloped land, not to mention their own back yards. Beyond built-up areas, of course, the choice widens, as country lanes and pathways, agricultural fields, orchards, meadows, valleys, lake and stream banks, wooded areas, hillsides, mountain tops, and beach fringes yield their harvest.

Certain particularly good places for foraging wild edibles have been given an odd name by those who like to excavate, develop, pave and generally rearrange the environment. They are called "waste places": pockets of land that have been disturbed but not built upon. Here the absence of trees and the freshly turned earth allow an abundance of new growth. It seems to me that no land is wasted if it supports growing vegetation, is home to insects and is visited by birds, reptiles, amphibians and mammals. Perhaps we should call them "resource places," or even "useful places." But whatever the name, and wherever you find them (they are often close to civilization), check them out for plants that you can use for herbal drinks. During an overnight camp stop at one such place in British Columbia's Cariboo region, I counted ten plants that would yield both food and drink.

Where Not to Harvest

Parks, of course, will have many plants suitable for wild drinks, but remember that picking or disturbing anything in a park is illegal—and that includes wilderness parks. Avoid collecting along nature trails too, and at campsites or scenic places where the natural beauty is enhanced by the wild growing vegetation.

Margins of agricultural fields and orchards may well offer a variety of usable plants, but it would be well to find out first whether they have been sprayed with pesticides or chemical fertilizers. Such toxins may not be poisonous on the planted crops but may be harmful if ingested as a tea made from leaves that have been sprayed. The same goes for lawns and gardens which may have had chemicals applied. Care should also be taken when gathering from the roadside, or from railway or power line rights-of-way — often areas that are extensively sprayed with herbicides.

What to Harvest

The first rule for eating anything from the wilds is KNOW IT IS EDIBLE. Take the time to examine the plant thoroughly before picking any part of it for consumption. To the beginner, one plant often looks very much like another. Learn to recognize the plant as a whole, not just its flower or leaf, and get to know how it appears when a young sprout and when fully mature. Walking over the same trail at monthly intervals, paying attention to each species of plant, is a good way to learn the different stages of their growth. Teach yourself to recognize a plant stunted from poor soil or in full growth from rich.

The second rule is IF IN DOUBT, LEAVE IT OUT. It is not worth risking a stomach ache (or something worse), especially if you are out camping. If you are unsure in the identification of any species, don't use it. Remember, too, to use only the recommended parts of plants; otherwise you could run into trouble. We all know, for instance, that the stems of garden rhubarb are edible and delicious, and yet the leaves are deadly poisonous. In general, the young leaves of a plant make the best tea, but in some cases the matured leaves are required for a good flavour. Such plants will be specified in the pages that follow.

Try to harvest only plants that are abundant in the area. One or two plants may mean that the species is just getting started. Give it a chance to become well established. If a plant is rare in the area it is best not to risk killing it. Plants or flowers on the endangered species list are not included in this book.

Drinks made from roots have been included to make the book as complete as possible, but since taking the root destroys the plant, I strongly recommend that, unless you are faced with an emergency or survival situation, you avoid making drinks from plants of this sort—dandelions excepted! The same holds true, but to a lesser degree, for plants with rhizomes (roots that run horizontally beneath the soil surface). Taking a section of rhizome is less destructive than taking the root—but only if it is done carefully. In any case, take what you require without uprooting the whole plant, so that it can continue to grow.

How to Harvest

Choose a warm sunny day when leaves and flowers are not moist from dew or rain, and harvest only those plant parts not deformed or damaged by insects. A plastic bag is probably the best container as it can be stored in a pocket so easily. It is a good idea to keep at least one of these tucked in the pocket of every outdoor jacket you own—just in case.

Avoid the temptation to overpick: TAKE ONLY WHAT YOU CAN USE. Spread your picking among several shrubs or plants, and over different branches to minimize the damage to growth. A plant will hardly miss a leaf or two from a few of its branches, but stripping too many from the same place could seriously harm its development. Garden weeds are exempt from this rule, of course.

With respect for the growth of a single plant comes respect for the whole outdoors. Caring people will watch their footsteps to avoid crushing small plants or new life sprouting from the forest floor, especially in springtime. Branches in the way will be pushed to one side, not broken, to allow them to return to their original position. Nothing will be disturbed unnecessarily, and no litter of any kind will be left behind.

I like to remember, and pass on to others, the words of a hand-painted sign put up at the edge of one of the most beautiful beaches I know—Brady's Beach, near Bamfield, on the west coast of Vancouver Island:

> *Let it not be said*
> *To your shame,*
> *All was in its place*
> *Until* YOU *came.*

Making the Drinks

Preliminaries

Back at home or camp with your bag of collectibles, the next step is to empty the bags, one at a time if you have several, and go through the contents, discarding any undesirable material: dead leaves, grass, stems, leaves or berries in poor condition or damaged by insects. Check for small spiders, caterpillars or other hitchhikers. Don't kill them; just deposit them back outdoors where they belong.

Separate those plants that can be made into drinks while still fresh and those that must be dried before brewing. If you have gathered plants with which you can do either, brew some fresh and dry the rest. That way you can experience both and decide which you prefer.

Making Teas

Teas made with the fresh plant parts are the easiest and quickest of the drinks to prepare, which makes them ideal for hikers, campers, boaters and others away from home base. Crush the vegetation before steeping or simmering, to allow the natural flavours to escape more readily.

Most teas, however, require that the leaves or flowers be dried before using, and this is an important step in making successful teas from wild plants.

Drying

After a quick rinse in cold water, toss the plant materials in a tea towel to remove surplus moisture, then spread them one layer thick on newspaper. Multiple flower heads (such as yarrow) will dry more quickly if plucked from their stems and separated. Roots and stems will dry more evenly if the thicker ones are split to the size of the thinner ones, or are sliced or chopped. Berries are best dried on a cookie sheet with a lip.

Separate those that are in bunches, and remove the stems. Do whatever is required to allow air to circulate freely about the plant material.

Don't put leaves from two different plants on the same newspaper. When they dry and shrivel up, you may no longer be able to distinguish the species. If you have several different kinds of plants, it is a good idea to write the name of the plant in felt pen on the newspaper so that you will know which is which.

Lay the sheets of newspaper flat in a warm dry place where there is air movement and a minimum of dust. A food dehydrator is ideal, of course. Or you could make a drying rack by nailing bug screen onto a frame and hanging this over a stove or furnace, or setting it outdoors in warm weather. Plant material should not be dried in direct sunlight, however, as this causes loss of flavour and vitamin content.

Leaves, flowers, berries and roots are ready for storage *only when they are thoroughly dry*—that is, when they have become shrivelled and brittle. If any moisture remains, stored material will become mouldy and spoil. PARTLY DRIED LEAVES MUST NOT BE USED FOR TEA because certain species are toxic at this stage, even though quite safe when totally dry.

Storing

Once the plant parts are quite dry, they should be stored away. Glass jars with tightly fitting lids are ideal, especially because you can choose the size most suitable for the amount of material to be stored. Thoroughly wash and dry the jars and lids, eliminating any that have a lingering odour from their previous contents. Leaves and flowers can be stored whole, to be crushed just before brewing, or you can crush them prior to storage. The latter method will take up less space, but keeping them whole preserves the flavour better.

Be sure to label each jar as you fill it. Once dried and crumbled into a jar, green leaves all tend to look the same, and confusion comes easily. Stick-on labels are fine, but you can save this expense by putting a printed card inside the jar, with the name facing out through the glass. This removable card also ensures that the empty jar won't be refilled with another type of leaf and

Above, a drying rack built from bug screen, an old
picture frame and some cord; below, dried
wilderness plants in labelled jars

left wrongly labelled. Store the containers in a cool dark place, never in sunlight.

Steeping

The method most often used for brewing teas is steeping:

1. Measure the required amount of water into a saucepan (or any container with a lid) and bring to a full boil.

2. Either drop in the measured plant parts, put the lid on and remove from stove or fire, or

3. Put the plant parts directly into a warmed teapot and add the desired amount of water.

4. Let the container or teapot sit awhile, usually five or ten minutes until the tea is brewed—just as you would with store-bought tea.

Remember: the longer it brews, the stronger the tea, so if your brew is too strong for your taste, or too weak, adjust the steeping time with the next pot.

Simmering

A few teas need to be simmered to really bring out the flavour. Once the leaves or flowers have been dropped into the boiling water, reduce the heat or move the pan to the edge of the fire, maintaining a very slight boil.

Serving

Because much of the tea-making material will float on the surface, you will need to strain the tea before it is served. Outdoors people may be satisfied to skim off the bits with a stiff leaf.

True herbal-tea lovers will enjoy many of the newly dis-covered flavours just as they are, but for those with a sweet tooth, honey may improve the taste. Do be adventurous and try mixing different teas, or, if you are in your kitchen, add a little cinnamon, nutmeg, clove or a dash of almond or vanilla extract, depending on the type of drink. Try the well-known squeeze of

Iced tea from wild mint, mountain ash lemonade
and a tingling glass of crab apple juice
for refreshment in warm weather

lemon juice, grated orange peel or a sprig of mint (wild, of course). Try turning a tasty hot tea into an iced tea by refrigerating, pouring into a tall glass, and throwing in some suitable bright berries or fresh wild flowers along with the crushed ice. Use the flowers of the plant from which the tea is made.

Making Coffees

Wilderness coffees are not "instant coffees," since they are not immediately ready for use the way some teas are. They take more time to collect—especially the roots—and roasting is a prerequisite. Nevertheless, they are well worthwhile making on a camp trip or for use in the home.

Roasting

Roots for making coffee need not be peeled but should be thoroughly cleaned before roasting. Slice thick roots into pieces of equal size so that they will roast evenly. Lay the sliced roots (or the seeds, if you are making coffee from seeds) on a baking sheet so that they will roast evenly, and roast in a slow oven (250°F) for an hour or two, depending on size, until crisp. The camper can roast them directly over a fire, but stands a good chance of too much heat burning the would-be coffee. Better to manufacture a simple oven from a sheet of aluminum foil. (Such an oven is also very good for baking biscuits.)

Allow the thoroughly roasted coffee to cool, and then grind it. Away from kitchen facilities, grinding can be done by pounding with a smooth hard stone, or using a bottle like a rolling pin on a piece of wood or flat stone.

Brewing

Once the coffee is roasted and ground, brew it as you would the store-bought kind by percolating or using the drip method, but measure a larger amount. Outdoors, I believe the best way to make any kind of coffee is to bring the water to a boil, toss in a pinch of salt, add the ground coffee and let simmer for ten minutes. Strain before serving. Honey and cream can be added,

Dandelion roots are roasted, above, in a foil
campfire oven, and ground, below, on a
rock with a smooth stone

but try the natural flavour first. Don't compare wild coffees with supermarket or gourmet blends, but enjoy them for their own distinctive flavour.

Making Other Drinks

Besides teas and coffees, the wilderness provides several other excellent beverages that are well worth trying. Berries lend themselves to cordials, and these can be used in a variety of ways. There are very good "lemonade" drinks that are ideal for the thirsty hiker, and fun for small children to make since they require no boiling water. Farther on in the book you will also find a sarsaparilla-like drink and a spicy hot drink.

With some experimenting, you can make interesting cocktails and cooling summer drinks from the lemonades and cordials by adding gin or vodka and a sprig of something wild and attractive. There need be no limit to your imagination and no end to the delight of discovering new and tasty thirst quenchers.

Preserving

Enjoyment of natural teas, coffees and other drinks need not end with the season. Having discovered which of the wild drinks you prefer most, gather a surplus of their ingredients for future use. With correct drying and storage, they will last through the year to the next season when you can go out and replenish your store.

Sipping fragrant clover or strawberry tea in January will take you back to that picnic one hot summer day by the lake. A lemonade party-punch made with sumac seeds will recall that hike up the mountain side and the rich, red glow of the sumac in the warm September sun. At Christmas, a hot spicy drink made from manzanita berries will remind you of the lazy days boating through coastal islands, when you scrambled ashore over sun-warmed rocks to pick the berries.

For an unusual gift to someone who enjoys herbal teas, put the dried leaves in an attractive glass storage container that has a tightly fitting lid. Create a fancy label with a simple illustration of the wild plant, give its common name and botanical name, date and place collected, and decorate the container with a ribbon.

Beyond Wild Drinks

Keep notes on the drinks you most enjoyed and the variations you tried out; keep tabs on what you mixed with what, and in what proportions, so that you can make it again if it was successful. But don't stop at drinks from the wild. Go on to discover herbal medicines and a range of good, healthful eating through wild edibles: the salad greens, vegetables, seasonings and fruits of mountain, meadow and valley. Then explore the shoreline for the tasty edibles from the intertidal zone.

You may even want to go beyond foods and learn about fibres and other raw plant materials that can be useful to the outdoor person in a variety of ways. But wherever you go and whatever you collect, do it with sensitivity to the environment.

First Nations peoples offered a prayer of thanksgiving to the spirit of the tree or shrub before harvesting from it, believing that to respect the resource was to ensure its abundance in future years. That says it all.

WILD MINT
TEA
Mentha arvensis

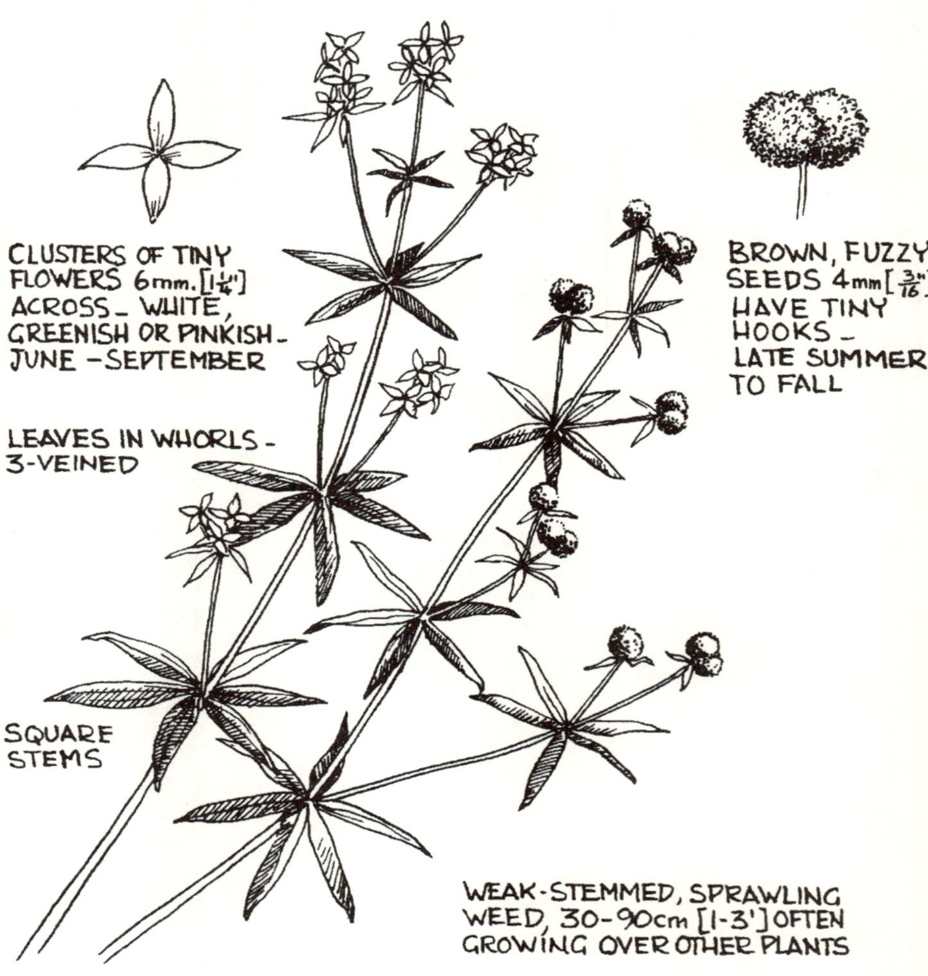

CLUSTERS OF TINY
FLOWERS 6mm. [1¼"]
ACROSS _ WHITE,
GREENISH OR PINKISH _
JUNE _ SEPTEMBER
LEAVES IN WHORLS _
3-VEINED
SQUARE
STEMS
BROWN, FUZZY
SEEDS 4mm [3/16"]
HAVE TINY
HOOKS _
LATE SUMMER
TO FALL
WEAK-STEMMED, SPRAWLING
WEED, 30-90cm [1-3'] OFTEN
GROWING OVER OTHER PLANTS

Bedstraw
Galium aparine

Other Names

Cleavers
Goosegrass

Habitat

There are several species of this widely distributed plant, which grows from sea level up into high mountain ranges. Look for it in wooded or open areas, especially along stream banks and in other moist places.

Season

The pale flowers that bloom from June on into September give way to fuzzy green seeds which turn rich brown when mature.

Preparation

This is probably the best of the coffee-like drinks—and that is not surprising, since bedstraw is a member of the true coffee family. Gather a quantity of the seeds just as they have matured—that is, when they have just turned brown—and roast in a slow oven until dark brown and crisp. Grind and use these miniature coffee beans just as you would any other coffee. Campers can pour boiling water directly onto the ground seeds and simmer gently for 15 minutes.

Did you know...

English children toss lengths of this plant onto the back of a person's sweater or jacket as they pass, and secretly laugh at the trailing stems that cling to the clothing. This tenacity gives the nickname "cleavers." The name "bedstraw" comes from early times in Europe when quantities of a sweet-scented species were used for stuffing mattresses. Legend has it that the Christ child was laid on a bed of the dried, fragrant plant.

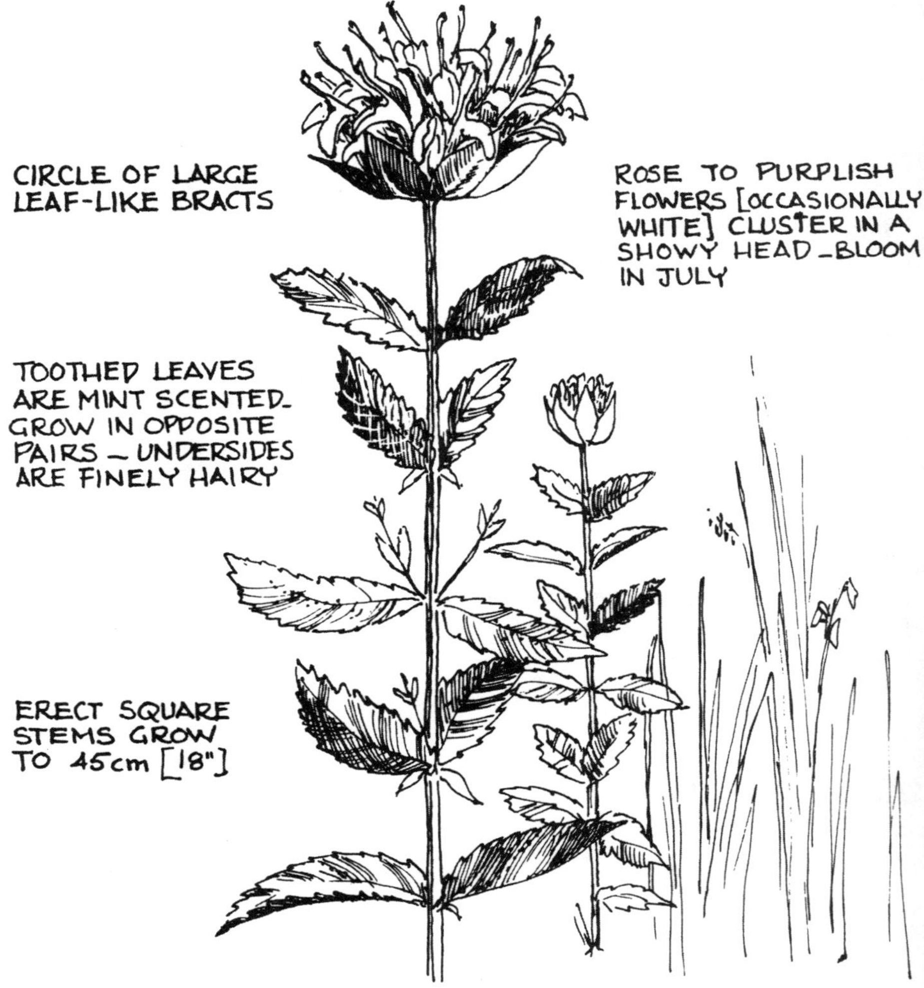
CIRCLE OF LARGE
LEAF-LIKE BRACTS

ROSE TO PURPLISH
FLOWERS [OCCASIONALLY
WHITE] CLUSTER IN A
SHOWY HEAD—BLOOM
IN JULY

TOOTHED LEAVES
ARE MINT SCENTED—
GROW IN OPPOSITE
PAIRS — UNDERSIDES
ARE FINELY HAIRY

ERECT SQUARE
STEMS GROW
TO 45cm [18"]

Bee Balm

Monarda menthaefolia

Other Names

Wild bergamot
Horsemint

Habitat

Bright patches of this plant of
the central and southern British
Columbia interior will surely attract
the wanderer's attention. Thriving
in pine forests, open and often rocky
places at low altitudes, it is a
member of the mint family.

Season

Bee balm is available throughout the
summer.

Preparation

The fresh or dried leaves will make
an excellent and refreshing tea. For
a three-cup pot, crush a handful of
fresh leaves, or use two teaspoons of
the dried, crumbled leaves, and
steep for 7 minutes.

Did you know...

Dried and powdered leaves of bee
balm sprinkled on meat and other
foods act as an insect repellent. Try
it around your camp.

FLAT SEEDS 1·3cm [½"]
LONG, HAVE STRONG
FENNEL FLAVOUR

BALLS OF YELLOW FLOWERS
ARE POISED ON STEMS
LIKE UMBRELLA SPOKES -
WHOLE FLOWER HEAD UP
TO 8cm [3"] WIDE

NO LEAVES ON FLOWER STEMS

L. NUDICAULE HAS
OVAL LEAFLETS TO
8cm [3"]. LONG FLOWER
STEMS GROW FROM
30-90cm [1-3'] HAVE
SWELLING AT HUB

L. TRITURNATUM HAS SLENDER
LEAVES AROUND 6cm [2½"]
LONG, SINGLY AND IN THREES

PLANT GROWS 30-60cm [1-2']
HIGH, OFTEN WITH FLOWER STEM
TWICE HEIGHT OF LEAVES

Biscuitroot

Lomatium triternatum & *Lomatium nudicaule*

Habitat

Most of the half dozen or more species of lomatium in the West seek out dry, exposed places, frequenting open meadows, rocky roadside banks and talus slopes.

Season

The two lomatium species illustrated here greet the spring with their bright yellow pom-pom flowers. They continue blooming until July, and late summer brings clusters of pungent seeds.

Preparation

The flowers, leaves and stems of these plants can be used for a tea of unusual flavour. Gather mostly leaves (sparing the flowers for others to enjoy), dry them and steep the crushed leaves for 10 minutes. A heaped teaspoon should be about right for each cup of boiling water.

Did you know...

First Nations peoples and the early settlers of eastern Canada ground the inner part of the thick taproot into flour, mixed it with water and flattened the dough into long cakes, which were sun-dried or oven-baked. A hole was made in the centre so the cakes could be lashed to a saddle or hung from roof beams for storage. They were said to taste like stale biscuits, hence the name "biscuitroot."

One old name for the plant, "Indian consumption plant," comes from the Native peoples' use of the ground seeds as a medicine for the dreaded consumptive diseases introduced by colonists.

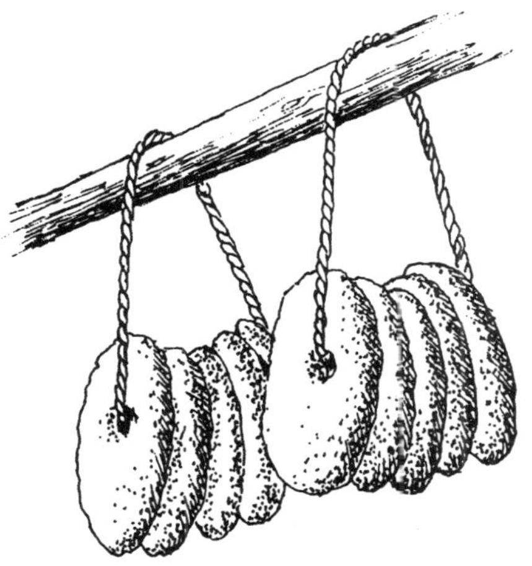

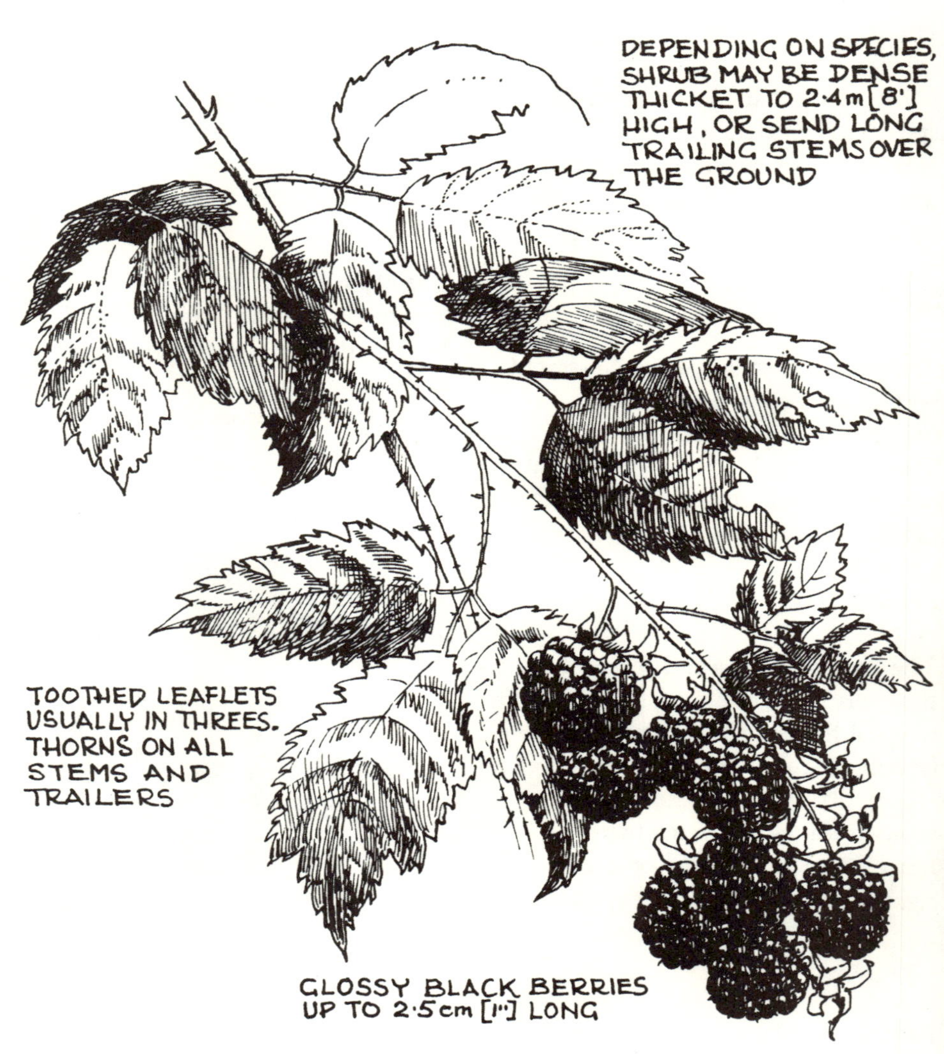

DEPENDING ON SPECIES,
SHRUB MAY BE DENSE
THICKET TO 2.4m[8']
HIGH, OR SEND LONG
TRAILING STEMS OVER
THE GROUND

TOOTHED LEAFLETS
USUALLY IN THREES.
THORNS ON ALL
STEMS AND
TRAILERS

GLOSSY BLACK BERRIES
UP TO 2.5cm [1"] LONG

Blackberry

Rubus vitifolius & other species

Habitat

Surely everyone is familiar with blackberries, which sprawl in lavish profusion over fences, beside fields and ditch banks, along railway and road banks, and even in back lanes and gardens or vacant lots.

Season

The lush black fruit of late summer can generally be picked through August and September, with late stragglers often still ripening in October. Leaves for tea are at their best when they are old and turning red. Dried leaves remaining on the plant in winter are also good for tea.

Preparation

You can use blackberries to make a cordial for a delicious cold drink. Simmer the ripe berries with a very little water until soft enough to be crushed with a potato masher. Add honey or brown sugar to taste. Strain the pulp through a jelly bag; cool and store the juice in the refrigerator. Serve cold with a squeeze of lemon juice, or mix half and half with apple juice and add a dash of rum. Or mix the cordial with tonic water or soda for a fine thirst quencher.

You can also use dried or fresh blackberry leaves for a tea. Use a handful of fresh old leaves, crushed, or two teaspoons of dried crumbled leaves for each cup of boiling water. (Watch out for the sharp spines on the backs of the leaves.) Sweeten to taste.

In addition to using blackberries for the usual desserts, use them to make a luscious jam (page 129) or jelly.

Did you know...

People often brew excellent home-made wines from blackberries. The wine matures quickly and the fruit imparts good colour and flavour.

Coast Salish First Nations people on Vancouver Island used the vines of trailing blackberry for ritual scrubbing. Other groups in the interior of British Columbia used the juice to stain wood, hides and other materials.

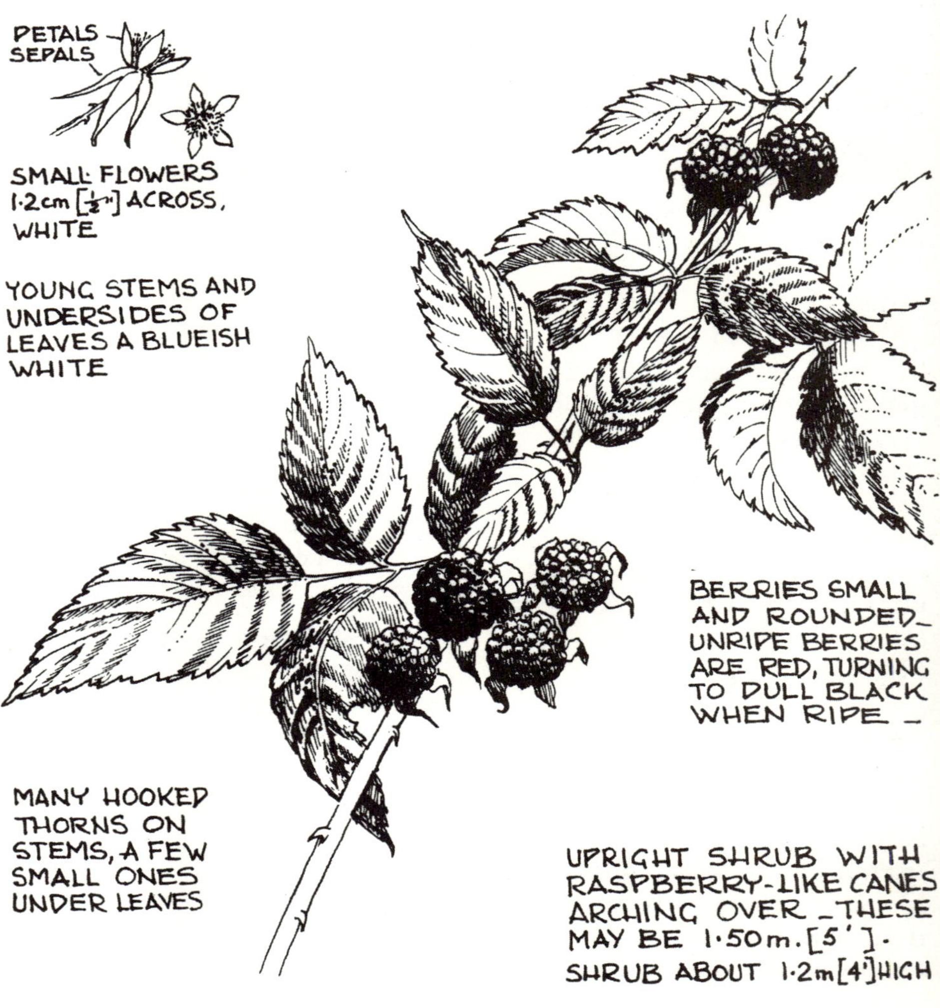

PETALS
SEPALS
SMALL FLOWERS 1·2cm [½"] ACROSS, WHITE
YOUNG STEMS AND UNDERSIDES OF LEAVES A BLUEISH WHITE
BERRIES SMALL AND ROUNDED_ UNRIPE BERRIES ARE RED, TURNING TO DULL BLACK WHEN RIPE _
MANY HOOKED THORNS ON STEMS, A FEW SMALL ONES UNDER LEAVES
UPRIGHT SHRUB WITH RASPBERRY-LIKE CANES ARCHING OVER _THESE MAY BE 1·50m. [5']. SHRUB ABOUT 1·2m [4'] HIGH

Blackcap
Rubus leucodermis

Other Names

Black raspberry
Wild loganberry

Habitat

A widespread shrub often found in logged off and cleared areas, this member of the rose family also thrives in moist bottomland, open woods and along the edges of ditches.

Season

A perennial, the blackcap puts out fresh young leaves in the spring. The berries are ripe from late summer to fall.

Preparation

Here is another dual-purpose plant. For a good tea, put half a cup of thoroughly dried young leaves in a teapot, add boiling water and allow to steep for 5 to 8 minutes. Sweeten to taste. (The fresh green leaves can also be steeped for tea.)

For an unusual cold drink, pack a jar full of ripe berries, then add vinegar to the brim. Seal the jar and allow to stand for four weeks. Strain the resulting juice through cheesecloth, add sugar, a little water and ice cubes. Delicious.

Did you know...

Both the Thompson and Lillooet First Nations people used blackcap juice as a red stain for wood and other materials.

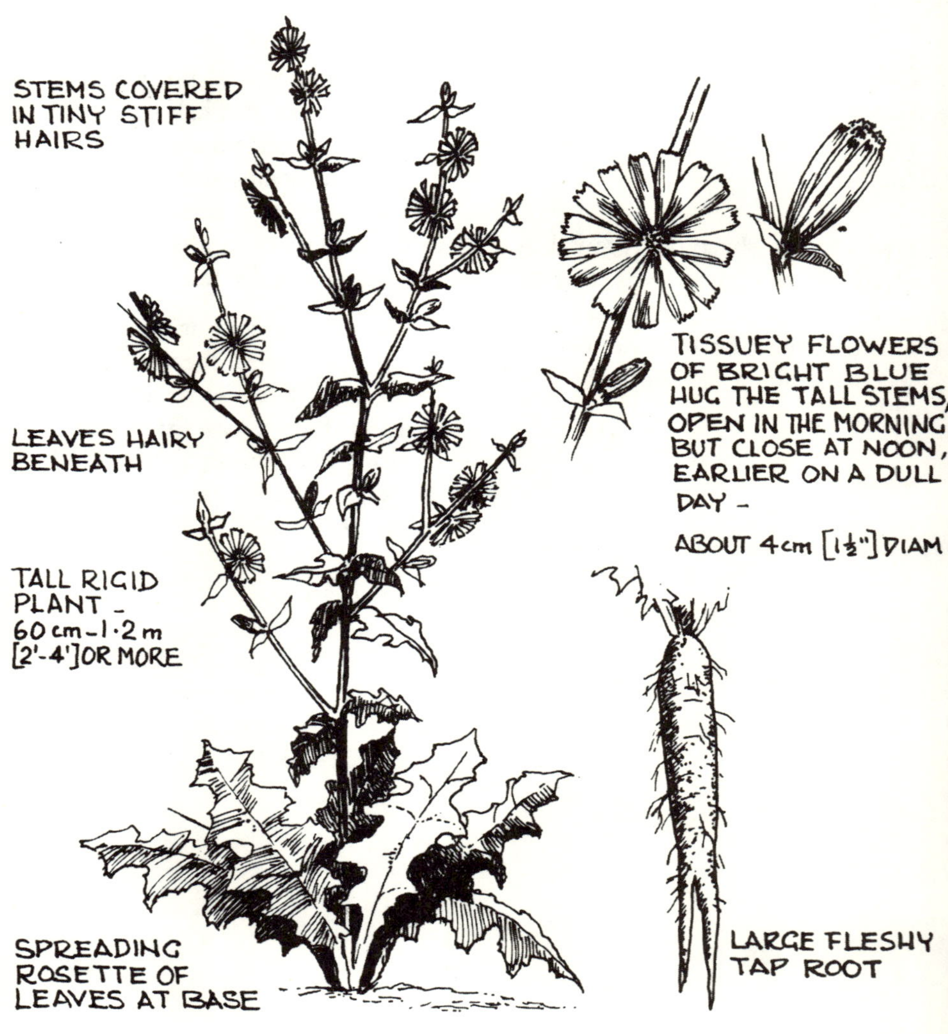

STEMS COVERED
IN TINY STIFF
HAIRS

LEAVES HAIRY
BENEATH

TALL RIGID
PLANT -
60 cm - 1·2 m
[2'-4'] OR MORE

SPREADING
ROSETTE OF
LEAVES AT BASE

TISSUEY FLOWERS
OF BRIGHT BLUE
HUG THE TALL STEMS,
OPEN IN THE MORNING
BUT CLOSE AT NOON,
EARLIER ON A DULL
DAY -

ABOUT 4 cm [1½"] DIAM.

LARGE FLESHY
TAP ROOT

Blue Sailors

Cichorium intybus

Other Names

Chicory
Chicory lettuce

Habitat

Scattered or in patches, tall stands of blue sailors add a decorative splash to roadsides, fields and open sunny places.

Season

These bright flowers bloom from July to September, but the roots are best gathered well before the plant blooms, or after they have been touched with frost.

Preparation

Thoroughly clean the fleshy roots, roast them in a slow oven until crisp, then grind according to method of use. You may use this as you would a regular coffee, or as an additive for extra flavour. As the generic and common names imply, this plant contains chicory. Unless it is a matter of survival or dire necessity, choose not to make a coffee of blue sailors; they are perennials, and taking the roots destroys them.

Instead, why not make a tea from the flowers? Steep a heaping teaspoon of the dried blossoms for each cup of water, adding honey to taste.

Did you know...

This immigrant plant came originally from Europe and the Near East. Curiously, the petals of the sky blue flowers keep regular hours, opening at 7:00 A.M. and closing again at noon (standard time), even on a sunny day. Bees know this timetable and visit only during open hours. '

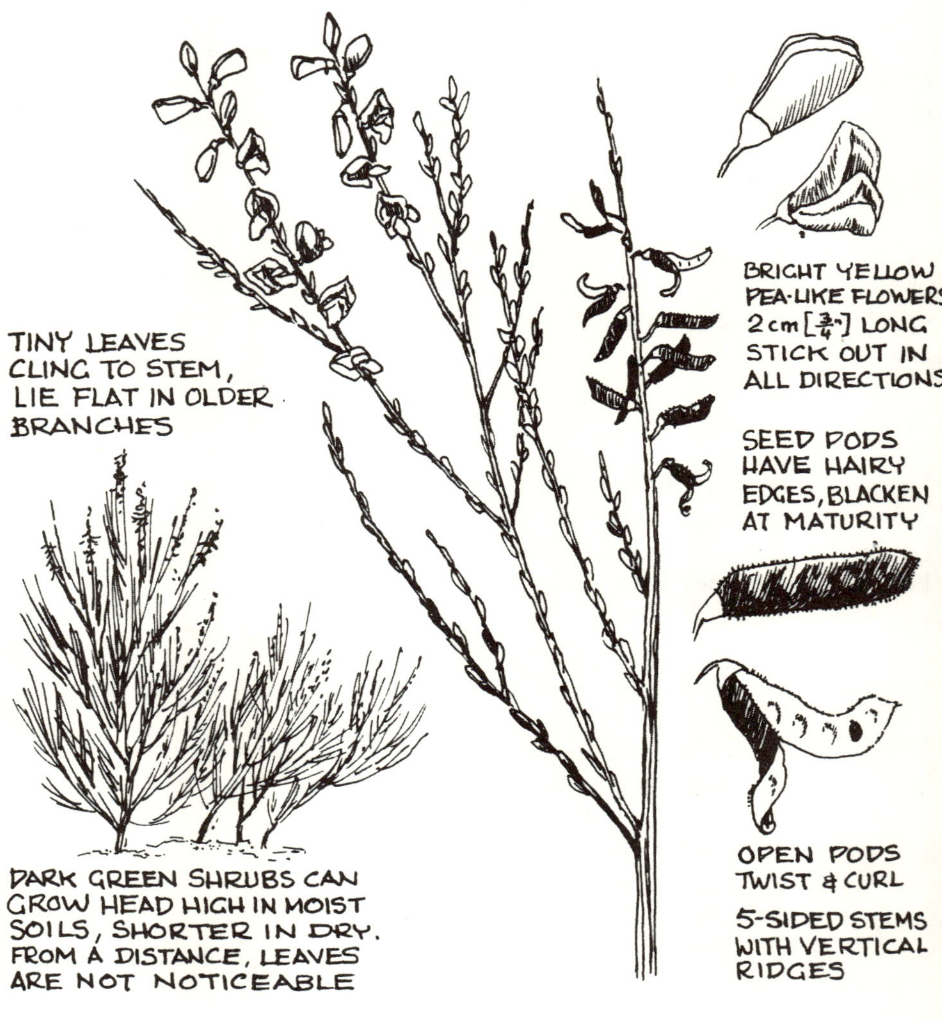

TINY LEAVES
CLING TO STEM,
LIE FLAT IN OLDER
BRANCHES

DARK GREEN SHRUBS CAN
GROW HEAD HIGH IN MOIST
SOILS, SHORTER IN DRY.
FROM A DISTANCE, LEAVES
ARE NOT NOTICEABLE

BRIGHT YELLOW
PEA-LIKE FLOWERS
2 cm [3/4"] LONG
STICK OUT IN
ALL DIRECTIONS

SEED PODS
HAVE HAIRY
EDGES, BLACKEN
AT MATURITY

OPEN PODS
TWIST & CURL

5-SIDED STEMS
WITH VERTICAL
RIDGES

Scotch Broom

Cytisus scoparius

Habitat

Scotch broom is a shrub found in abundance in vacant lots, along roadsides, and on railway embankments and sunny slopes. Their mass of yellow blooms makes a brilliant springtime splash.

Season

Although Scotch broom blooms early, the seeds do not ripen until October, when their black pods burst open with a sharp crack, scattering the contents. For a beverage, collect the pods before they reach this stage, while the seeds are still soft—about late August.

Preparation

Gather a quantity of seed pods and shell them like peas. Spread the seeds over a shallow pan and roast in a medium-hot oven. Finely grind the roasted seeds and use the drip method to make an alternative to coffee. Don't expect a real coffee flavour, but learn instead to enjoy the taste of an interesting new drink. WARNING: Fresh Scotch broom pods and seeds should not be eaten or used raw, as they contain toxic alkaloids.

Did you know...

In the mid-nineteenth century, a captain of the Royal Scots Greys who had settled at Sooke on Vancouver Island planted a dozen Scotch broom seeds given to him by the British Consul of the Sandwich Islands (now known as Hawaii). Only three of them grew into plants, but over the years their seeds have spread rapidly, establishing the shrub far afield. The seeds can remain viable for eight years and more.

The long, slender and pliable branches lend themselves for use as a base for a Christmas wreath. Make a circular form by bending a bunch of branches, wrapping them with twine or wire. Continue adding branches and wrapping until you achieve the desired size, overlapping the two ends to form a circle. Sprigs of fir, cedar or holly can easily be bound onto this base to cover the form. Add a string or wire loop to facilitate hanging up.

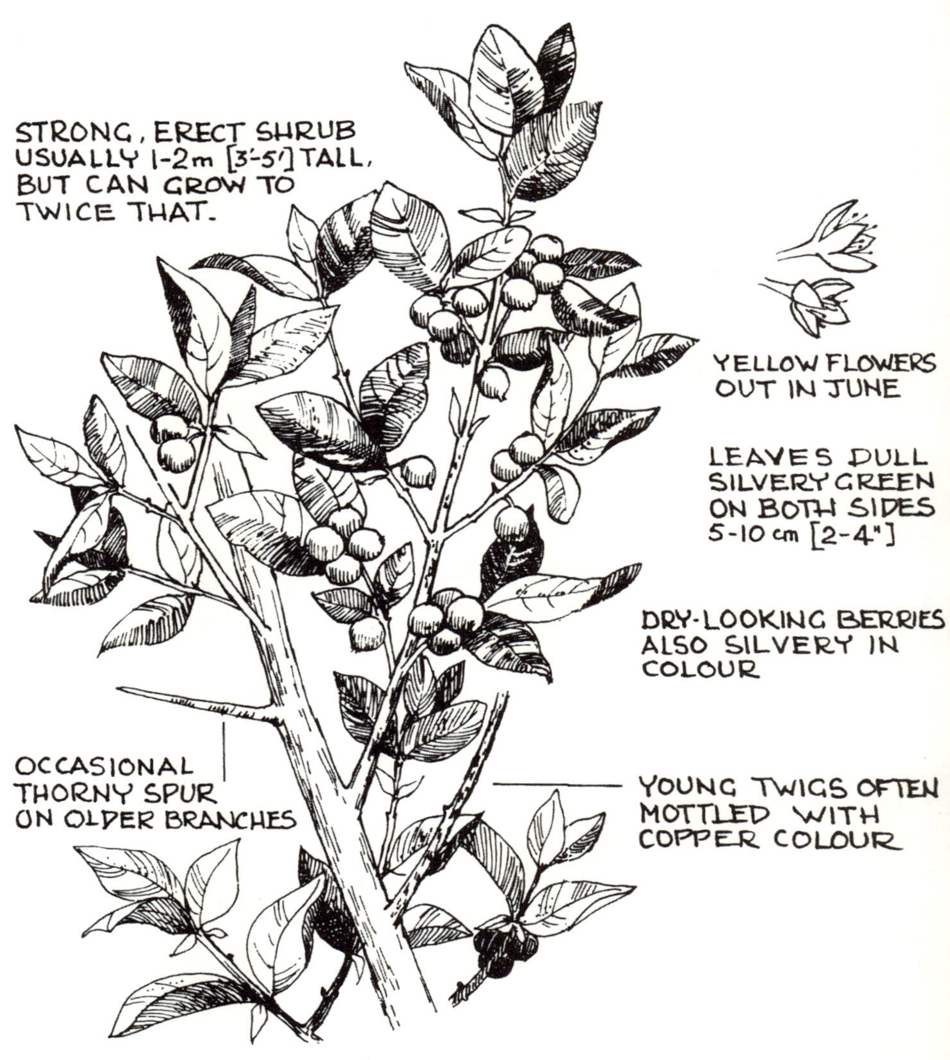

STRONG, ERECT SHRUB USUALLY 1-2m [3'-5'] TALL, BUT CAN GROW TO TWICE THAT.
YELLOW FLOWERS OUT IN JUNE
LEAVES DULL SILVERY GREEN ON BOTH SIDES 5-10 cm [2-4"]
DRY-LOOKING BERRIES ALSO SILVERY IN COLOUR
OCCASIONAL THORNY SPUR ON OLDER BRANCHES
YOUNG TWIGS OFTEN MOTTLED WITH COPPER COLOUR

Buffaloberry
Shepherdia argentea

Other Names

Silver buffaloberry
Silverberry

Habitat

Canoeists, kayakers and river-rafters will often come across shimmering groves of this shrub on the back channels of large creeks and rivers in warm, dry environments. It inhabits stream edges, too, making itself quite conspicuous because of its glistening silver foliage and stems.

Season

Ripening in August and September, even the berries are a dry, silvery colour.

Preparation

Wash the berries well, crush them in cold water and allow them to stand for 10 minutes, then strain to make a pleasant and tart lemonade drink. If your palate finds it too bitter, add a little brown sugar. Use about one tablespoon of berries to a cup of water—more if you prefer it stronger.

Did you know...

Folk tales recall that, in pioneering days, travellers crossing the prairies made a sauce of these berries for their buffalo steaks. This, or the fact that the berries were grazed by plains bison, would account for the common name.

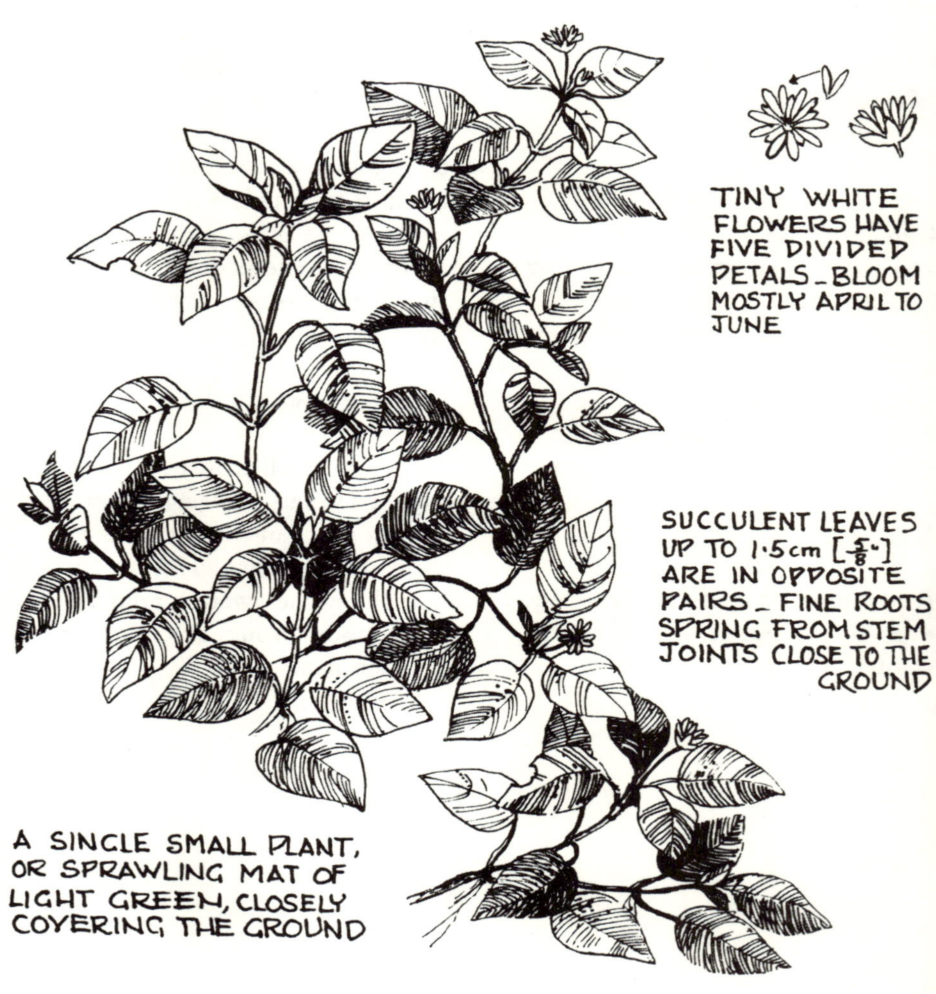

TINY WHITE
FLOWERS HAVE
FIVE DIVIDED
PETALS _ BLOOM
MOSTLY APRIL TO
JUNE

SUCCULENT LEAVES
UP TO 1·5cm [$\frac{5}{8}$"]
ARE IN OPPOSITE
PAIRS _ FINE ROOTS
SPRING FROM STEM
JOINTS CLOSE TO THE
GROUND

A SINGLE SMALL PLANT,
OR SPRAWLING MAT OF
LIGHT GREEN, CLOSELY
COVERING THE GROUND

Chickweed

Stellaria media

Other Name

Starwort

Habitat

There are many species of chickweed, but this is the pesky one, bothersome to gardeners because it so quickly establishes itself in freshly turned soil. Find it in your garden, by dirt roads, on compost heaps, in vacant lots and even at construction sites— anywhere there is moisture and open or partial shade, from sea level to 600 metres {2000 feet}.

Season

The plant can be used at any time and has a long growing season. In mild climates it continues to thrive throughout the winter. It blooms mostly from April to June.

Preparation

Gather up a small quantity of these weeds, rinse the dirt from the fine, white roots, and spread the plants out whole for drying. To make an attractive green tea, crush the entire dried chickweed plant and, using a teaspoonful or more per cup of water, steep for 10 minutes.

Did you know…

As well as making a good green tea, dried chickweed added to a biscuit mix gives it both colour and flavour.

PLANTS GROW TO ABOUT
30 cm [12"] HIGH, FORMING
LOOSE CLUSTERS.

LEAVES IN THREES, APPLE
GREEN WITH WHITISH
PATCHES.

FLOWER HEADS 2·4 cm
[1"] MAY BE PURPLE,
PINKY RED OR WHITE,
BLOOM FROM LATE
JUNE TO AUGUST, AND
SOMETIMES LATER.

Clover

Trifolium

Other Names

Sweet clover
Red clover
Purple clover
Trefoil

Habitat

About twenty species of clover are likely to be found almost any-where—meadows, roadsides, hill-sides, vacant lots, agricultural fields and so on. The plants often grow in extensive patches.

Season

The flowers bloom in July and August. The best tea is made from large flower heads, particularly the red, pink and purple ones.

Preparation

Clover heads should be dried before using, but the oven method is not recommended here. Instead, dry them at room temperature for three or four weeks. When drying is complete, pull out each individual flowerlet and discard the stem. To make tea, steep in the usual way, using one table-spoon for each cup of boiling water. Try adding a slice of lemon, some dried rose hips, wild mint or blue-berry juice for a distinctive flavour—and sweeten with clover honey, of course.

Did you know...

Northwest Coast First Nations peoples ate the roots of several species of clover. The women dug up great quantities of these with their digging sticks, steaming and roasting the roots in various ways according to tribal or local custom.

FRAGRANT WHITE
BLOSSOMS FROM
MAY TO JUNE ON
STRAGGLY TREE
UP TO 9m [30']

SHARP, STRONG
SPURS ON BRANCHES
2·5-5·0cm [1"-2"]

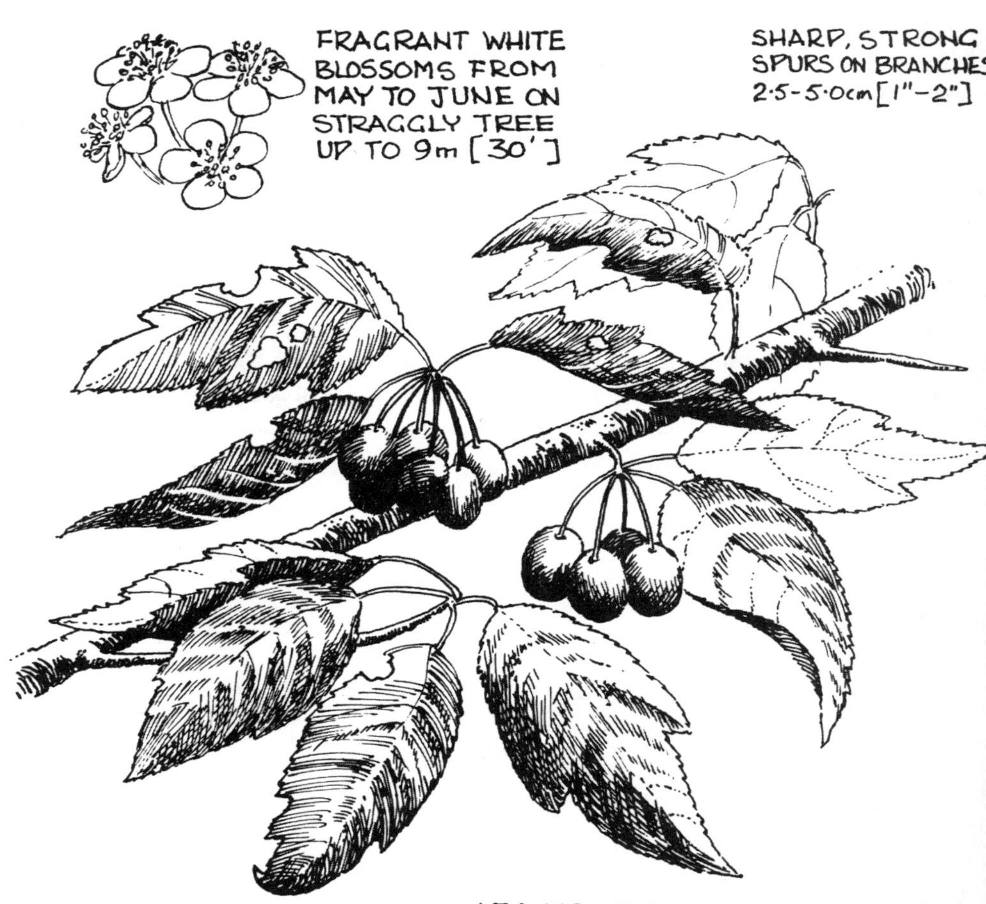

IN SEPTEMBER -
BUNCHES OF YELLOW TO
REDDISH OBLONG APPLES

1·3cm [½"] LONG

LEAVES HAVE A VARIETY OF SHAPES
WITH VARYING LOBES BUT ALL ARE
FINELY TOOTHED WITH PROMINENT
VEINS

AVERAGE LENGTH 6·3cm [2½"]

Pacific Crab Apple
Malus fusca

Other Names

Oregon crab apple
Western crab apple

Habitat

Forming dense thickets or growing as a single tree in the open, the wild crab apple clings to Pacific coastal areas, preferring moist valleys and stream banks. It is often abundant along low ocean frontage. Because of its clusters of small fruit, the crab apple is sometimes mistaken for a wild cherry.

Season

Springtime fills this tree with clusters of fragrant white blossoms that eventually turn into small green fruit. By late summer and fall, the fruit ripens to a warm yellow and bronze colour, and can be gathered by the handful.

Preparation

Remove all the stems and wash the fruit. Simmer in water to cover until soft, then mash. Add honey to taste. Strain through a jelly bag or fine sieve and chill. This juice makes a refreshing drink. For an especially tasty cordial, add a dash of cinnamon or nutmeg, or squeeze in the juice of half an orange.

You can also use crab apples to make a delicious jelly (page 129).

Did you know...

First Nations people mashed crab apples with salal berries and dried them in flat cakes for winter use. In addition, they used the hard, sharp spur wood from a tree branch, attaching it to a wooden shank to make a fish hook. With a little modification, the strong spurs on crab apple branches make excellent pegs, useful for craftspeople who work with wood.

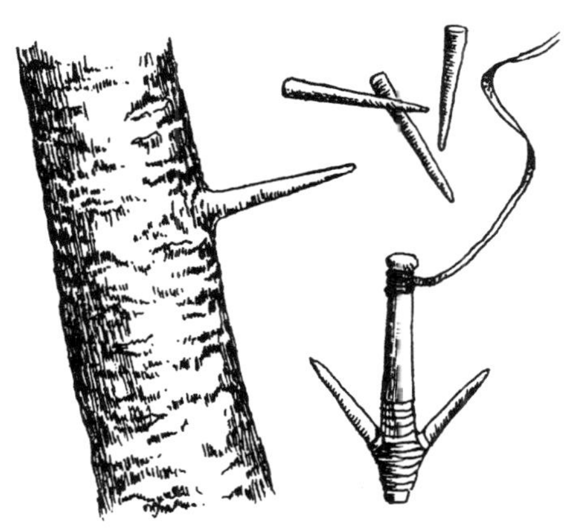

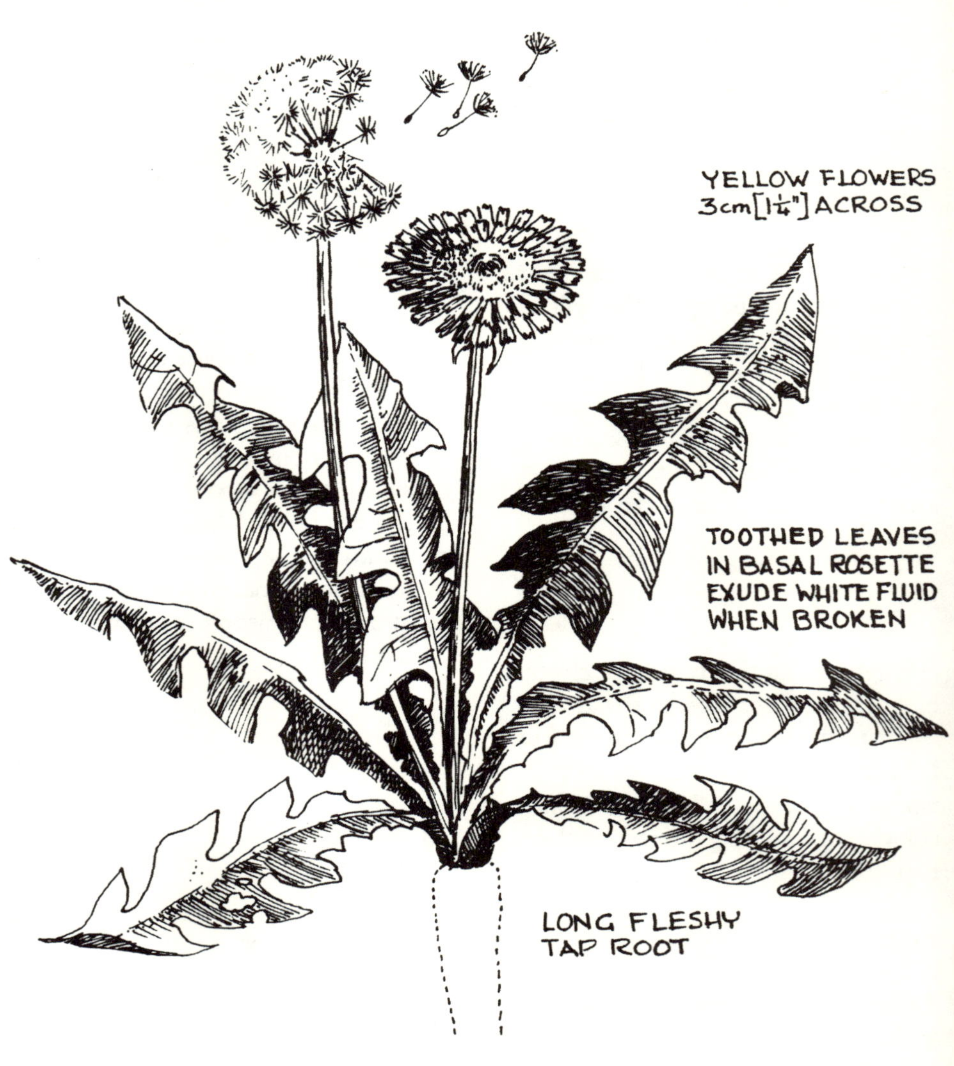

YELLOW FLOWERS
3cm[1¼"] ACROSS
TOOTHED LEAVES
IN BASAL ROSETTE
EXUDE WHITE FLUID
WHEN BROKEN
LONG FLESHY
TAP ROOT

Dandelion

Taraxacum officinale

Other Names

Lion's tooth
Pis-a-lit
Blowball

Habitat

The habitat of the dandelion need hardly be discussed, so familiar is this weed to everyone—especially gardeners. Harvesters should be aware that the richer the soil in which it grows, the bigger the root.

Season

The roots are best dug in early spring, well before the flowers appear, or in the fall after they have had time to replenish themselves. They are even better after a frost, but try them at other times, too.

Preparation

This is the one plant nobody minds digging up. Use a long trowel or shovel to take out the whole root; otherwise, it will break. Collect plenty. Cut off the tops, wash the roots well and remove the small wiry rootlets. Split thick roots in half or in quarters so that all are roughly the same thickness. Roast on a cookie sheet in a slow oven—or over a camp fire—for about two hours, until crisp and brown. Coarse-grind the roasted roots in a coffee grinder or with a rolling pin on a board, or between two stones if you are camping. Steep two teaspoons of the ground root per cup of boiling water, or use a percolator. This makes a light brown, reasonably good coffee drink with an interesting flavour.

To make a tea, pour one pint of boiling water over a good handful of well-washed leaves and petals. Steep for 5 to 10 minutes, strain and serve.

You can use dandelion buds in cooking. Sauté young buds for 2 or 3 minutes in a little butter, then fold them into an omelette. Garnish with crumbled bacon. For decoration, place a couple of dandelion flowers at the side of the plate.

Did you know...

There are over one thousand species of dandelion around the world. The common name is derived from the French *dent de lion*, which means "tooth of the lion," a good description of the jagged edges of the leaf.

Weavers use the bright yellow flower heads to make a yellow dye for wool.

FLAT, POINTED NEEDLES, A
LICHTER GREEN BENEATH,
ABOUT 2cm [¾"] LONG, ON
ALL SIDES OF STEM, LIKE A
BOTTLE BRUSH — SOFT TO
THE TOUCH, NOT SPIKY

TREE FORM IS TYPICAL
CHRISTMAS TREE SHAPE. BARK
OF OLD TREES DEEPLY FISSURED

SOFT, MATURE CONES
5–7.5cm [2–3"] DROP TO
THE GROUND IN FALL,
HAVE DISTINCTIVE THREE-
POINTED BRACTS BETWEEN
CONE SCALES

Douglas-fir
Pseudotsuga menziesii

Other Names

Douglas spruce
Oregon pine

Habitat

Douglas-fir (not a true fir) ranges over many areas and altitudes of central and southwestern British Columbia, Washington and Oregon. Such true fir species as alpine fir (high elevations), grand or balsam fir (southern British Columbia and Washington coasts), and amabilis fir (mainly coastal) are all suitable for making teas.

Season

The leaves remain on this evergreen conifer all year and can be collected any time, but choose the young ones if you can.

Preparation

For a refreshingly tasty drink, pour boiling water on a handful of fresh needles to make two cups of tea. Steep for 10 minutes or simmer 20 minutes for a stronger flavour. This tea is exceptionally rich in vitamin C.

Did you know...

The Douglas-fir is so named because it was first identified in 1829 by the famed Scottish botanist David Douglas. It is the most abundant tree in British Columbia and the tallest in Canada, growing to a height of 60 metres [200 feet] or more.

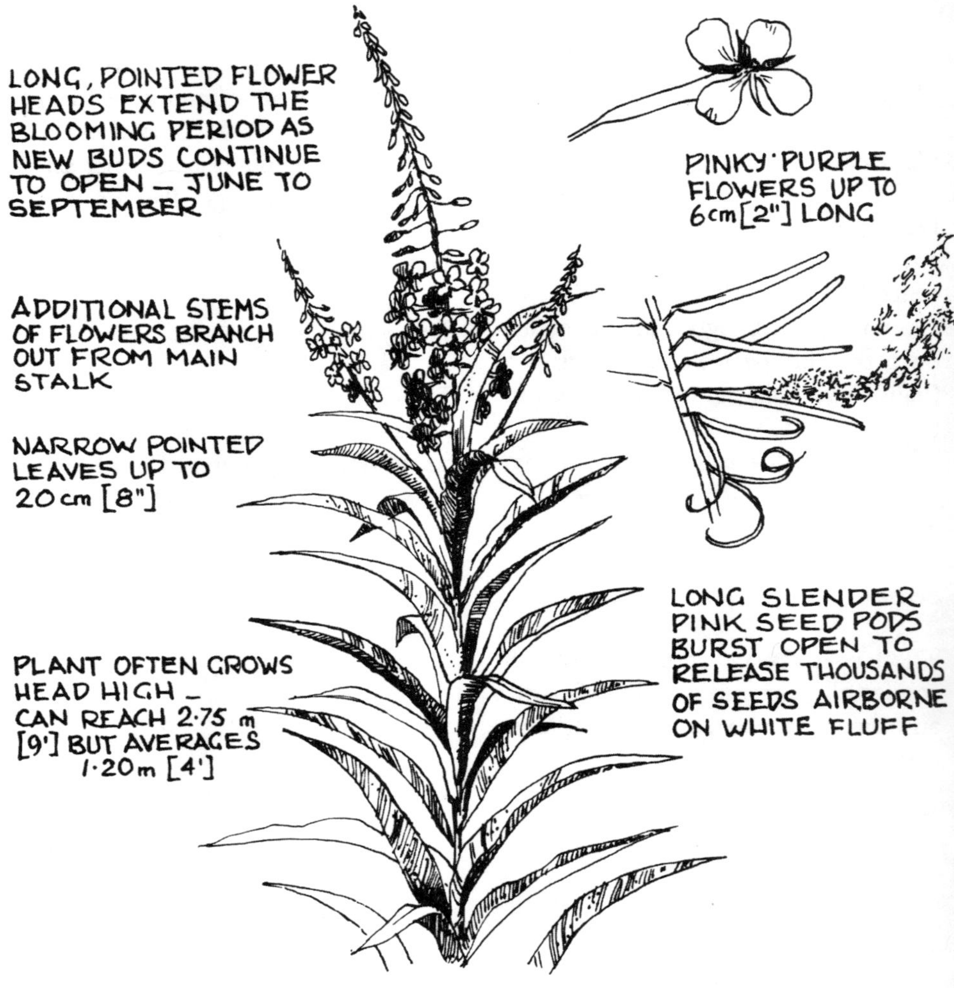

LONG, POINTED FLOWER
HEADS EXTEND THE
BLOOMING PERIOD AS
NEW BUDS CONTINUE
TO OPEN — JUNE TO
SEPTEMBER

ADDITIONAL STEMS
OF FLOWERS BRANCH
OUT FROM MAIN
STALK

NARROW POINTED
LEAVES UP TO
20 cm [8"]

PLANT OFTEN GROWS
HEAD HIGH —
CAN REACH 2·75 m
[9'] BUT AVERAGES
1·20 m [4']

PINKY·PURPLE
FLOWERS UP TO
6 cm [2"] LONG

LONG SLENDER
PINK SEED PODS
BURST OPEN TO
RELEASE THOUSANDS
OF SEEDS AIRBORNE
ON WHITE FLUFF

Fireweed

Epilobium angustifolium

Other Name

Willow herb

Habitat

Fireweed is especially abundant, as its name suggests, on land that has been burned over, such as clearings and logged-off hillsides. It also grows beside stream banks and in open woods, meadows and sunny places with fairly rich, moist soil. The more favourable the conditions, the taller it grows.

Season

Young plants shoot up in the spring and bloom from June to September. The leaves may be gathered anytime, but those picked before the plant has flowered make the best tea.

Preparation

You may use either fresh or dried leaves to brew tea. Crush a generous handful of green leaves (or two teaspoons of dried leaves) for each cup of boiling water and steep for 10 minutes. If this is not strong enough for your taste, blend it with other wild teas such as mint, rose hips, sheep sorrel or strawberry.

Try nutmeg and cinnamon, too, and add honey.

Did you know...

On the Northwest Coast, First Nations women sometimes mixed the soft white seed fluff with mountain goat hair or dog hair to weave blankets. Native people also made rope from the tough fibres of the tall, mature stalks.

After flowering, the seeds of firewood pods mature, releasing quantities of pappus, the fluff attached to the seeds. Gather up handfuls of this before the wind blows it away and use it for stuffing small toys.

The fibre in the outer stem of tall fireweed stalks can be peeled off, dried for storage and used much like nettle to provide material for basketry, small weavings, wrapping, binding and so on. Lengths of it can be twined into cordage (moisten before using).

SOMEWHAT LEATHERY,
HEART-SHAPED LEAVES
RISE IN PAIRS FROM NODES
OF FLESHY UNDERGROUND
RHIZOMES _ CREEPING ROOTS
SPREAD OVER FOREST FLOOR
TO BRING LARGE PATCHES OF
DEEP GREEN FOLIAGE

STRONGLY VEINED
LEAVES GROW TO
15 cm [6"] LONG,
HAVE SLIGHT
GINGER SCENT

LOWER EDGES OF
LEAVES & STALKS
SOFTLY HAIRY

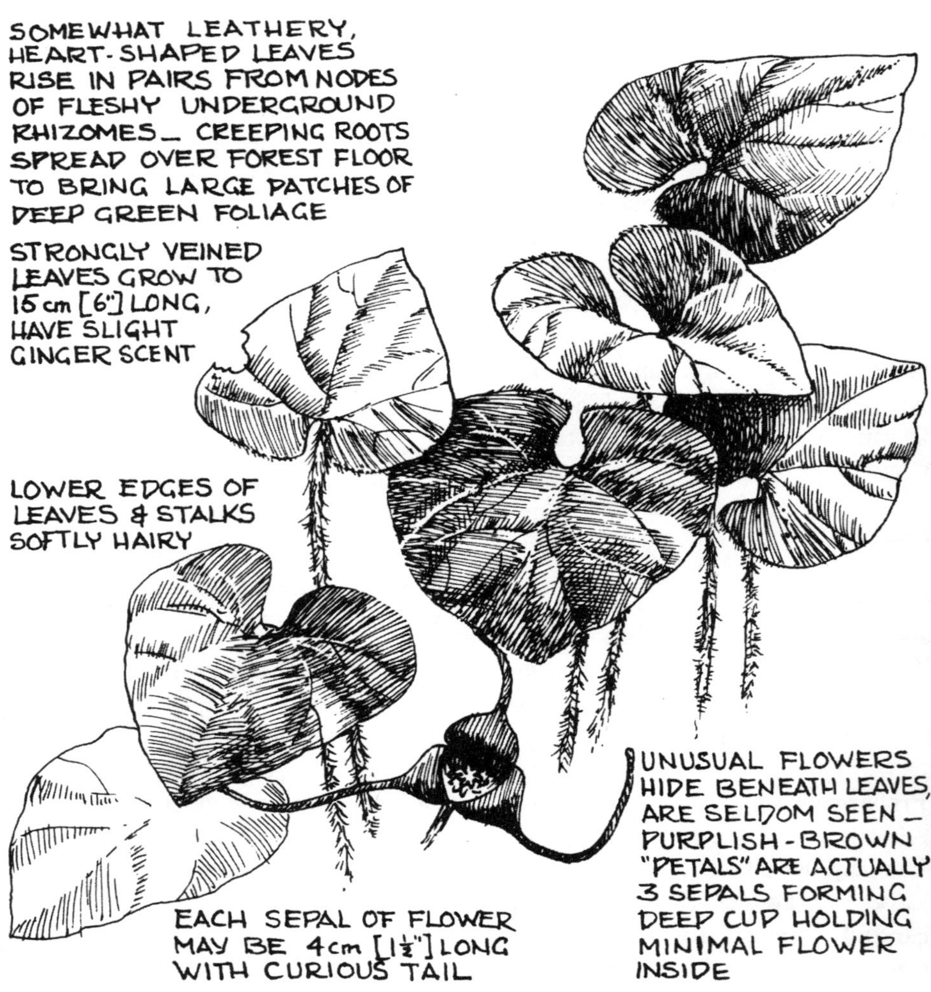

UNUSUAL FLOWERS
HIDE BENEATH LEAVES,
ARE SELDOM SEEN _
PURPLISH-BROWN
"PETALS" ARE ACTUALLY
3 SEPALS FORMING
DEEP CUP HOLDING
MINIMAL FLOWER
INSIDE

EACH SEPAL OF FLOWER
MAY BE 4cm [1½"] LONG
WITH CURIOUS TAIL

Wild Ginger

Asarum caudatum

Habitat

Wild ginger grows in moist, shady places. Its rhizomes favour the humus and moss of forest floor and stream edge, where it often remains unnoticed. Look for the distinctive heart-shaped leaves in rich bottomlands from the Cascade Mountains to the coast.

Season

This ginger is an evergreen, making it easy to locate at any time of year, especially in winter. Be careful not to confuse it with wild lily-of-the-valley (often found in the same habitat), which has a similar leaf but lacks the hairy stem. The latter is not an evergreen.

Preparation

Cut a few sections from the rhizomes, which run immediately beneath the surface of the ground and from which the paired leaves spring up. Remove and discard the leaves, wash the rhizomes and crush or chop into small pieces. Use two teaspoonfuls of the rhizome per cup of boiling water and simmer gently, or steep, for about 10 minutes. Sweeten with a little brown sugar to give the nearly clear liquid some colour. A dash of lemon will make this a very tasty hot drink. Try adding a small amount of ginger to other wild teas and juices to give them an extra zingy flavour.

To preserve ginger for later use, dry the stems (slicing the thicker ones in half lengthwise) until they are crisp and look like wire. To make a tea, simply break the dried stems into small pieces, simmering one teaspoonful per cup of water for 10 minutes.

Did you know...

People of the both the Thompson and Okanagan First Nations valued wild ginger for its pleasant aroma. They mixed it with absorbent sphagnum moss and used it for babies' bedding.

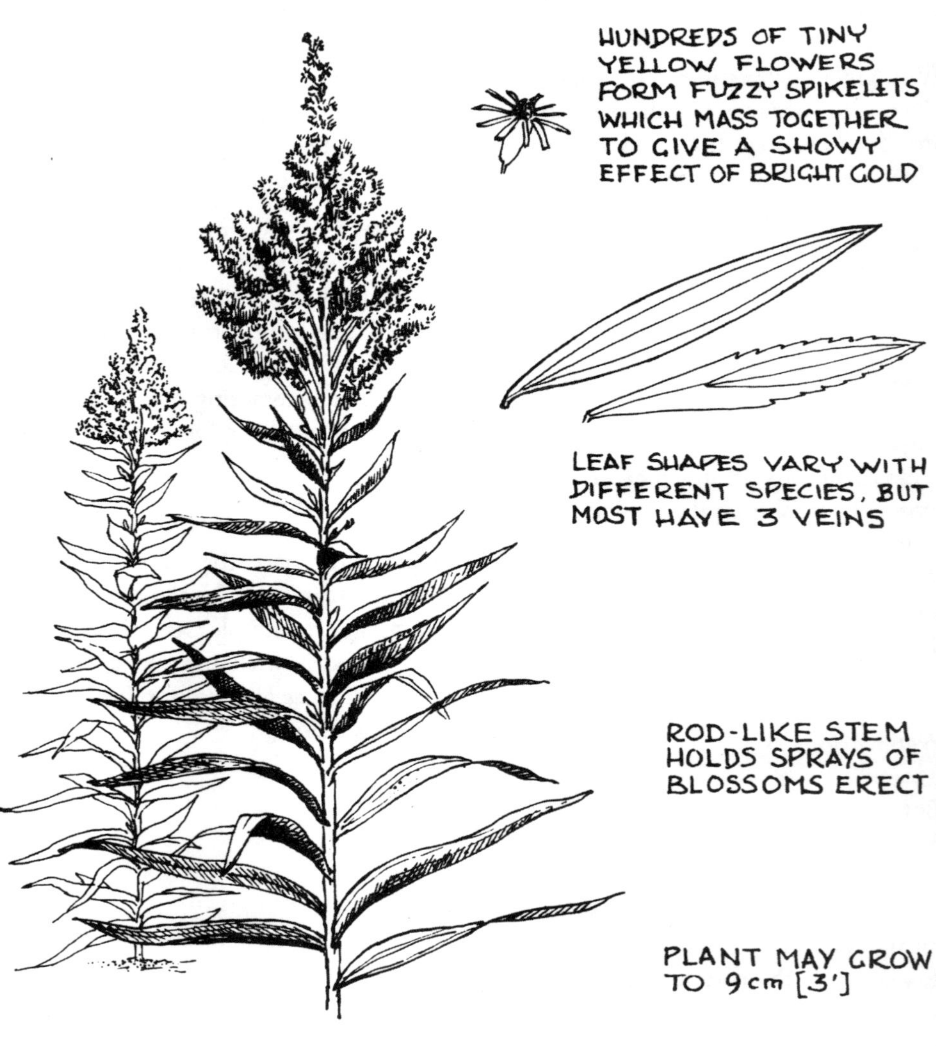

HUNDREDS OF TINY
YELLOW FLOWERS
FORM FUZZY SPIKELETS
WHICH MASS TOGETHER
TO GIVE A SHOWY
EFFECT OF BRIGHT GOLD

LEAF SHAPES VARY WITH
DIFFERENT SPECIES, BUT
MOST HAVE 3 VEINS

ROD-LIKE STEM
HOLDS SPRAYS OF
BLOSSOMS ERECT

PLANT MAY GROW
TO 9 cm [3']

Goldenrod

Solidago canadensis *& other species*

Habitat

Like torches of sunlight, the most common species of goldenrod brighten open places, road banks, edges of fields and other moist places that offer rich soil.

Season

Late summer into fall is the time to look for the golden brilliance of these flowers atop their stately stems, but the leaves are best picked in spring.

Preparation

Since you can use either the fully opened flowers or the young leaves to make a tea, choose to take the leaves only, allowing bees and other insects their right to the blossoms. Thoroughly dry the young leaves; use a heaped teaspoonful per cup of boiling water and steep for at least 10 minutes, adding a sweetener to taste.

Did you know...

The bright flowers of goldenrod are a traditional source for making a yellow dye that will not fade. In the past, people thought the pollen was a cause of hay fever, but research has proven that this is not so.

In winter, when goldenrod dies and the tall straight stalks have turned a tan colour and are still standing, they lend themselves to various other uses. Pick 15 or 20 stalks, snapping them off at varying lengths, and arrange them in a tall pottery vase or other container to create a dramatic winter eye-pleaser. The stalks are durable, though the fine flower stems are rather fragile. Or add the stalks to an outdoor salal arrangement (page 97).

You can also sand the dried stalks smooth and incorporate them into a woven mat or wall hanging.

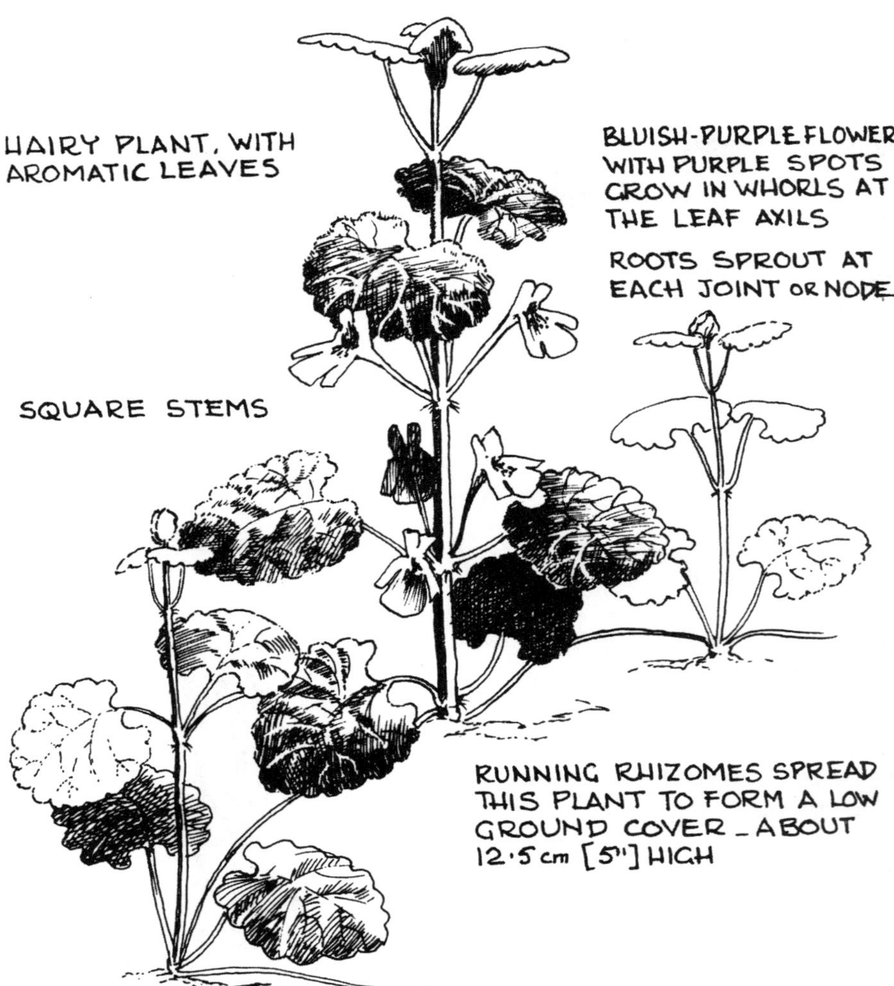

HAIRY PLANT, WITH AROMATIC LEAVES
BLUISH-PURPLE FLOWERS WITH PURPLE SPOTS GROW IN WHORLS AT THE LEAF AXILS
ROOTS SPROUT AT EACH JOINT OR NODE
SQUARE STEMS
RUNNING RHIZOMES SPREAD THIS PLANT TO FORM A LOW GROUND COVER – ABOUT 12·5 cm [5"] HIGH

Ground Ivy

Glecoma hederacea

Other Name

Gill-over-the-ground

Habitat

An inconspicuous plant that may pass unnoticed, even when in bloom, ground ivy favours moist, shaded places throughout the country. Look for it in woods and shaded gullies.

Season

This square-stemmed plant is a perennial; you can find it in late spring or summer sprouting runners to establish new plants.

Preparation

To minimize damage to this spreading ground cover, pluck only one or two leaves from several different plants. Dry them well, crush and brew for an unusual, aromatic tea.

Did you know…

Ground ivy has been known and used for tea in Europe for many centuries. It is a member of the mint family but lacks the familiar mint flavour.

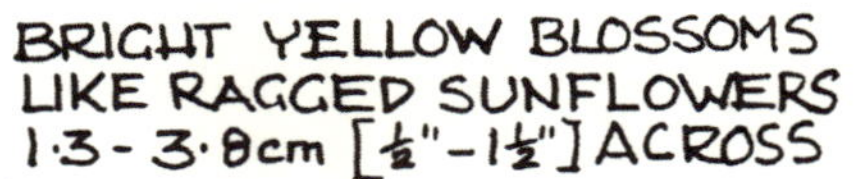

GUMMY GREEN BURR
BENEATH FLOWERS
BECOMES EVIDENT WHEN
PETALS DIE

LEAVES 2·5-5 cm [1-2"] LONG

BIG BUSHY PLANT
GROWS TO 75cm [2'6"]

LEAVES VARY WITH SPECIES

BASAL LEAVES
UP TO 20cm [8"]
IN LENGTH

THICK GUMMY
LEAVES TO 5cm [2"]
LONG — FOUND IN
DRY INTERIOR

Gumweed

Grindelia squarrosa, Grindelia oregana & other species

Other Names

Gum plant
Raisinweed

Habitat

Several gumweeds bear their bright yellow flowers, like miniature sunflowers atop gummy burrs, on bushy plants that vary their location. One species prefers open, dry places, often growing on freshly disturbed ground; another seeks the windswept surf spray of the coast; a third enjoys the warmth of the interior lands.

Season

These perennials put forth fresh green leaves in the spring; their showy blossoms in June continue through autumn and even into November.

Preparation

Gather the young leaves in the spring, or use the uppermost leaves later in the year. Gumweed leaves used fresh or dried make a pleasant tea. Crush a handful of the young greens and pour on boiling water; allow to steep 15 to 20 minutes.

Did you know...

The botanical name for gumweed honours the early Russian botanist David Grindel, who lived from 1776–1836.

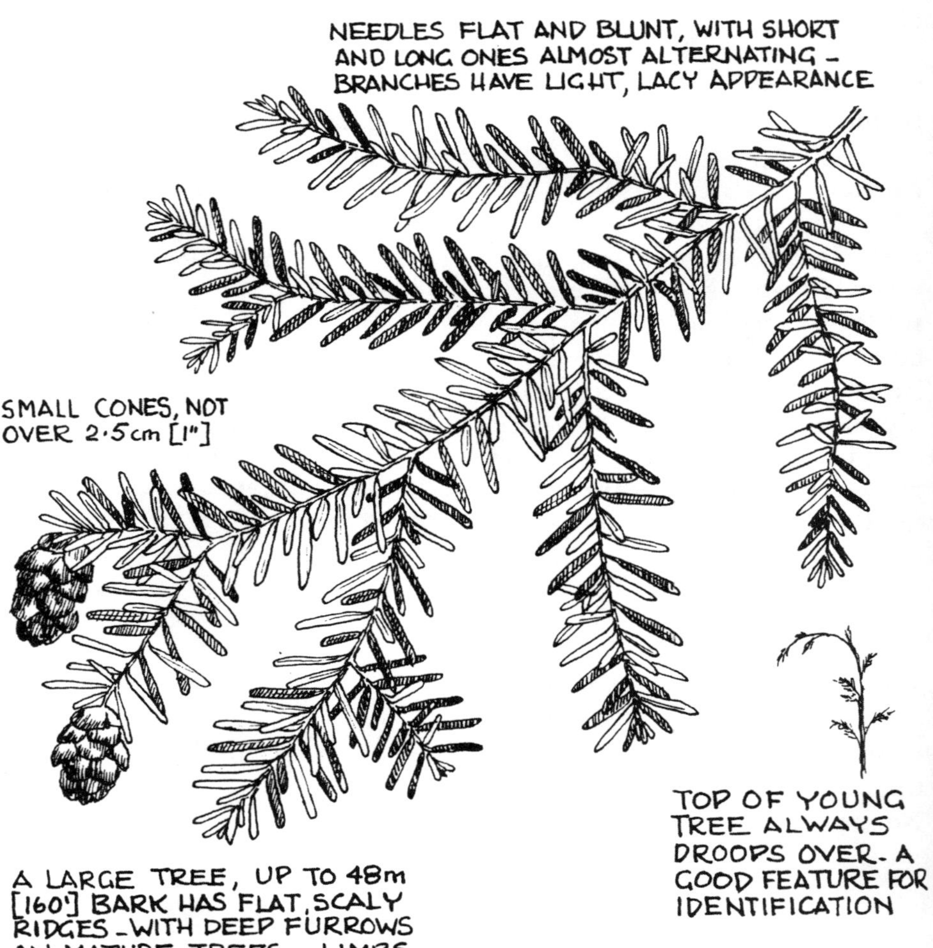

NEEDLES FLAT AND BLUNT, WITH SHORT
AND LONG ONES ALMOST ALTERNATING -
BRANCHES HAVE LIGHT, LACY APPEARANCE

SMALL CONES, NOT
OVER 2.5cm [1"]

TOP OF YOUNG
TREE ALWAYS
DROOPS OVER - A
GOOD FEATURE FOR
IDENTIFICATION

A LARGE TREE, UP TO 48m
[160'] BARK HAS FLAT, SCALY
RIDGES - WITH DEEP FURROWS
ON MATURE TREES - LIMBS
IRREGULARLY SPACED

Western Hemlock

Tsuga heterophylla

Habitat

This small-needled evergreen tree prefers to grow in moist shade. A conifer sprouting from the top of an old tree stump will most likely be hemlock. It is abundant in coast forests up to 850 metres [2800 feet], and in the interior wet belt up to 1500 metres [5000 feet].

Season

As an evergreen, hemlock is available year round, but its needles make the best tea in spring.

Preparation

Add a handful of the fresh young needles to two cups of boiling water and let simmer 20 minutes. Don't let the name deter you from trying this drink—it is not, and has no resemblance to, the poisonous hemlock that killed Socrates (*Conium maculatum*), a plant found in dry, gravelly places. Water hemlock, (*Cicuta occidentalis*) is a deadly poisonous plant of the marshes, but it too has absolutely no resemblance to western hemlock.

Did you know...

Hemlock was at one time a slow-selling product. When an enterprising lumber company promoted the wood as Alaska pine, its image changed. The wood became popular and the company prospered.

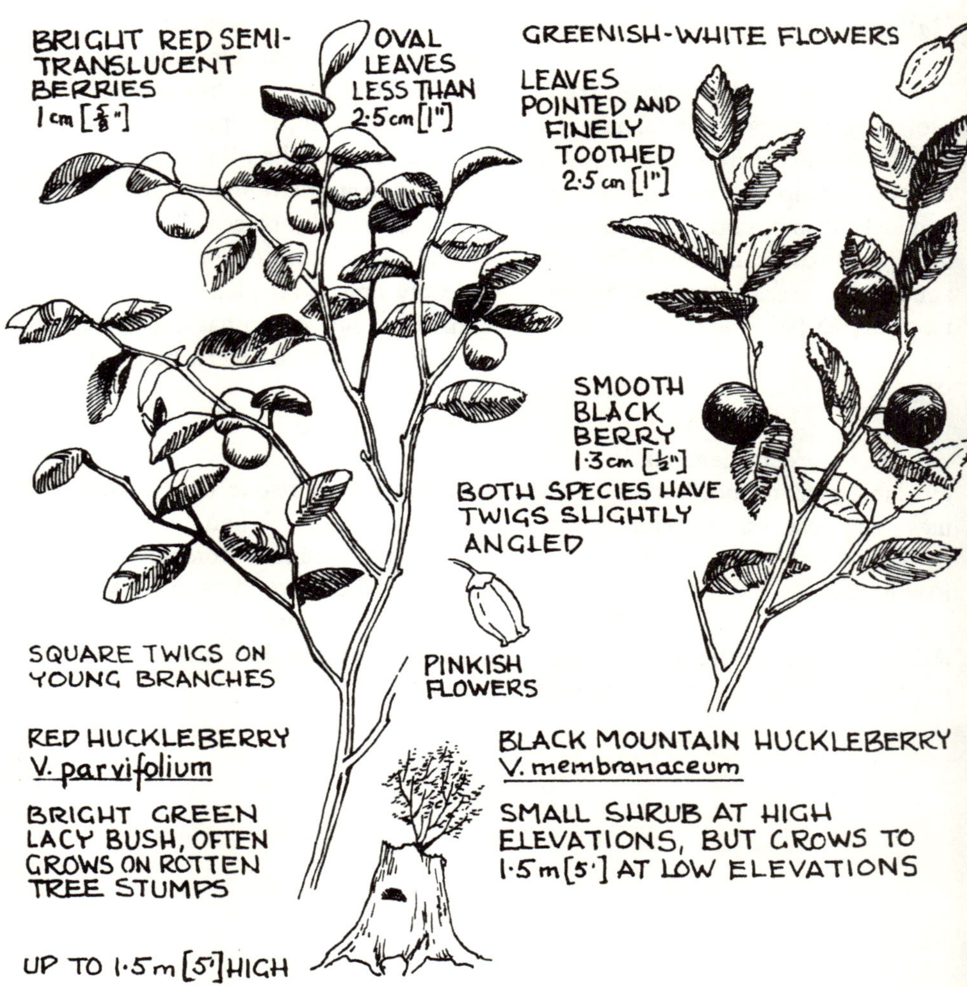

BRIGHT RED SEMI-TRANSLUCENT BERRIES
1 cm [⅜"]
OVAL LEAVES LESS THAN 2·5 cm [1"]
GREENISH-WHITE FLOWERS
LEAVES POINTED AND FINELY TOOTHED 2·5 cm [1"]
SMOOTH BLACK BERRY 1·3 cm [½"]
BOTH SPECIES HAVE TWIGS SLIGHTLY ANGLED
SQUARE TWIGS ON YOUNG BRANCHES
PINKISH FLOWERS
RED HUCKLEBERRY
V. parvifolium
BRIGHT GREEN LACY BUSH, OFTEN GROWS ON ROTTEN TREE STUMPS
UP TO 1·5 m [5'] HIGH
BLACK MOUNTAIN HUCKLEBERRY
V. membranaceum
SMALL SHRUB AT HIGH ELEVATIONS, BUT GROWS TO 1·5 m [5'] AT LOW ELEVATIONS

Huckleberry

Vaccinium parvifolium, Vaccinium membranaceum & other species

Other Names

Blueberry
Whortleberry
Bilberry

Habitat

Several varieties of these berries range from damp, shaded coastal forests to high mountain elevations in full sun. All are known by outdoor people, who pick them for use in pies, or to make jam and jelly (see page 130).

Season

The berries ripen in late summer and early fall, depending on the location.

Preparation

To make a tasty cordial, wash the berries, removing any leaves and stalks. Place in a saucepan with water to cover. Simmer just long enough for the fruit to break up, then crush with a potato masher to release the juice. Strain through cheesecloth, add honey and a few drops of almond extract to taste, then chill for a refreshing drink.

For a fragrant tea, pour three cups of boiling water over half a cup of berries—either fresh or dried—and steep for 10 to 15 minutes. Add honey to taste.

Alternatively, you can steep a handful of crushed green leaves in a two-cup teapot. The longer the steeping time, the stronger the flavour.

Did you know...

Bears like huckleberries too! Berry pickers should be aware that they may be intruding upon the territory of bears who, along with other creatures, have a greater right to the wild harvest than do humans. WARNING—take care and avoid a confrontation.

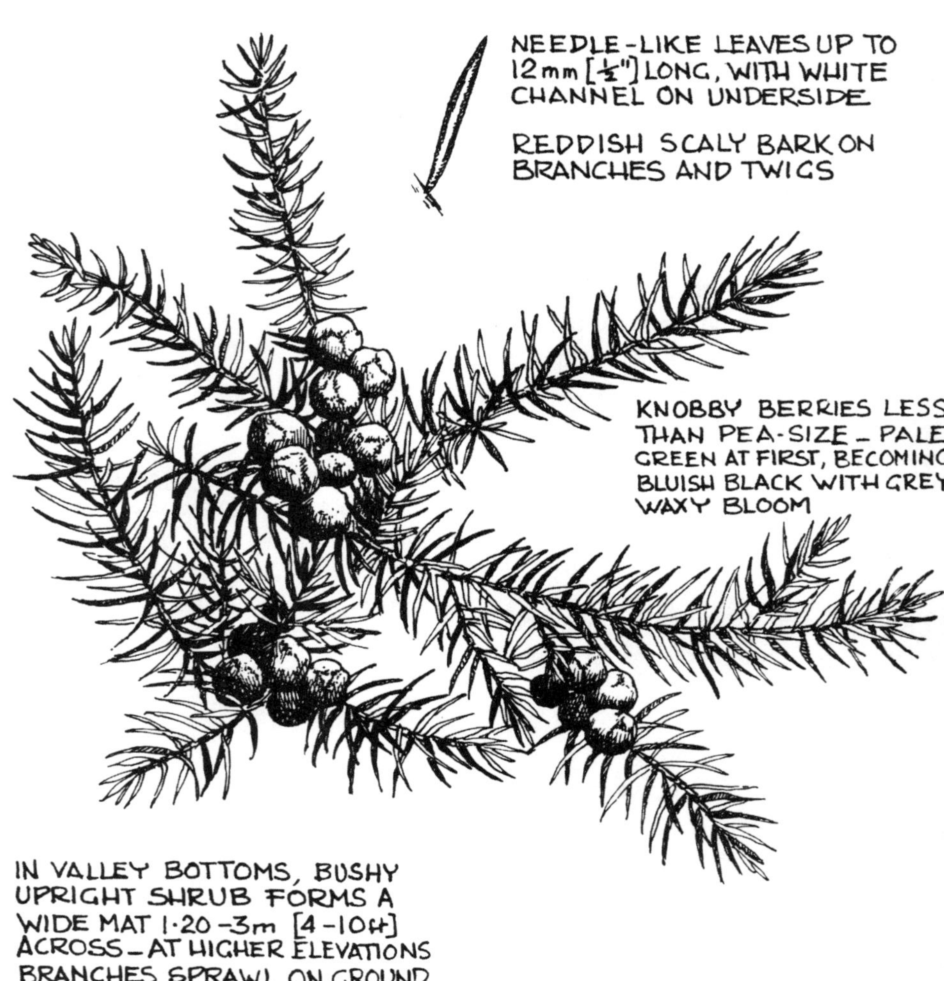

NEEDLE-LIKE LEAVES UP TO 12mm [½"] LONG, WITH WHITE CHANNEL ON UNDERSIDE

REDDISH SCALY BARK ON BRANCHES AND TWIGS

KNOBBY BERRIES LESS THAN PEA-SIZE — PALE GREEN AT FIRST, BECOMING BLUISH BLACK WITH GREY WAXY BLOOM

IN VALLEY BOTTOMS, BUSHY UPRIGHT SHRUB FORMS A WIDE MAT 1·20 –3m [4 –10ft] ACROSS — AT HIGHER ELEVATIONS BRANCHES SPRAWL ON GROUND

Juniper
Juniperus communis & other species

Habitat

The common or dwarf juniper has a wide altitudinal range; it inhabits open woods, valleys, dry hillsides, rocky bluffs and rock slides.

Season

Because the berry-like juniper fruit requires two seasons to mature, it can be picked throughout the year, as can its evergreen sprigs.

Preparation

Use both the twigs and the berries for an aromatic tea. Add one sprig of young leaves per cup of cold water and bring to the boil. Simmer, covered, for about 15 minutes. Add honey to taste.

The berries need to be dried before making a tea from them. Use one teaspoon of the crushed, dried fruit for each cup of boiling water, and steep for about 10 minutes. Honey improves the pungent flavour.

For a delicately different hot drink, try juniper berries roasted. Gather and dry the fully mature fruits, roast them in a slow oven until dark brown, then grind fine. Using one cup of water to one tablespoon of ground berries, pour on boiling water and allow to steep for a short while. Add a dash of nutmeg or cinnamon, and top with marshmallows or a splash of whipped cream—honey, too, if you wish. Other species of juniper can be used in the same way.

Did you know...

This is the species of juniper used in flavouring gin.

The "berries" of juniper are actually three scales fused into a cone, making this shrub coniferous.

The plant was of great value to First Nations peoples as a fumigant after sickness and death, and was also used to ward off ghosts and evil spirits. When the boughs are burned or boiled, they give off a strong but pleasant smell that acts as a deodorizer.

PINK BELL-LIKE FLOWERS
BLOOM MAY-JUNE

GROUND-HUGGING SHRUB
FORMS A MAT OR TRAILS

SHINY BERRIES OF BRIGHT
RED - 1·2cm [½"] AUGUST TO
LATE WINTER

SMALL LEATHERY LEAVES
LESS THAN 2·5cm [1"] LONG -
RED SHREDDY BARK ON STEMS

Kinnikinnick
Arctostaphylos uva-ursi

Other Names

Bearberry
Sandberry

Habitat

A ground cover with a delightful Indian name, kinnikinnick chooses well-drained areas, thriving on gravelly soil and rocky outcrops, sometimes trailing over rock or rotten logs in open forests and hillsides. It is widely distributed from sea level nearly to timberline.

Season

This plant is an evergreen. The leaves grow year round and the berries may linger for most of the winter – if deer and grouse have not devoured them.

Preparation

Here is another dual-purpose plant. The leaves, which have a high tannin content, make good tea when dried and then boiled for 15 minutes. The berries, also containing tannin, make a refreshing cold drink: add one cup of washed berries to one cup of water and two teaspoons of honey. Simmer until the fruit breaks up, then mash. Strain off the juice and chill before serving.

Did you know...

Kinnikinnick is an Algonkian word said to mean *smoking mixture* or *something to smoke*. The dried leaves were once used for smoking, or were mixed with trade tobacco. Early pioneers and country folk not only smoked a mixture of kinnikinnick leaves but also used them for the production of tannin. In Russia, tannin is still obtained from the plant.

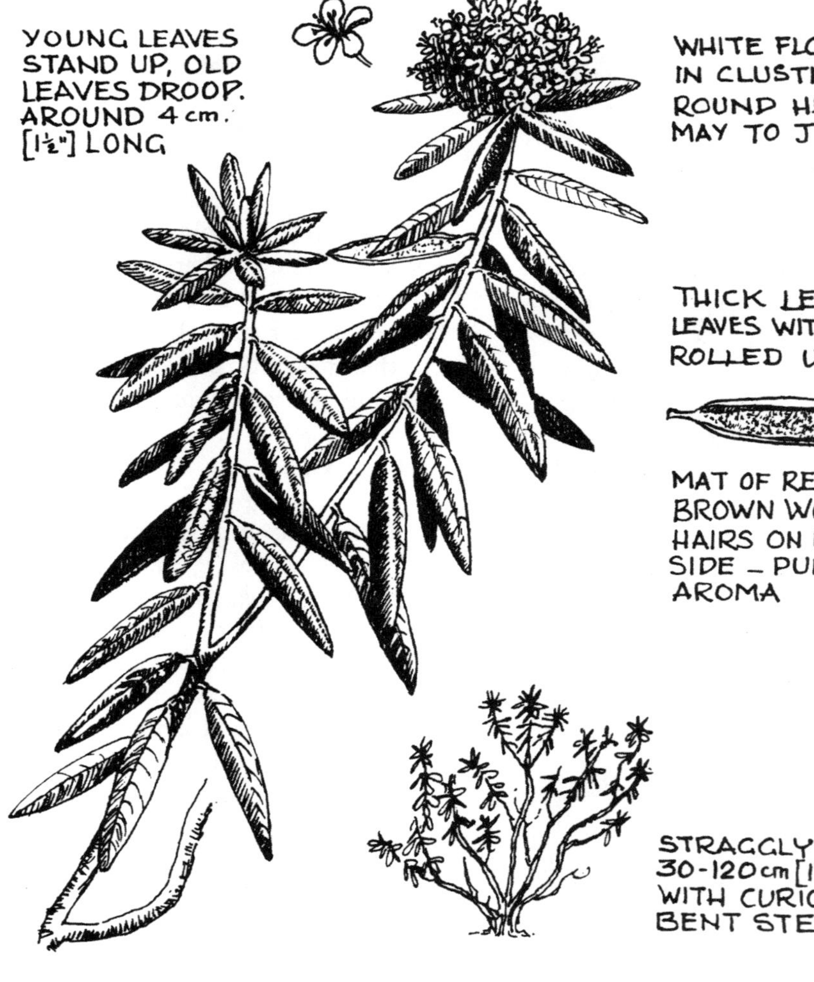

YOUNG LEAVES STAND UP, OLD LEAVES DROOP. AROUND 4 cm. [1½"] LONG
WHITE FLOWERS IN CLUSTERED ROUND HEADS. MAY TO JULY.
THICK LEATHERY LEAVES WITH EDGES ROLLED UNDER,
MAT OF REDDISH-BROWN WOOLLY HAIRS ON UNDER SIDE — PUNGENT AROMA
STRAGGLY SHRUB 30-120 cm [1'-4'] HIGH WITH CURIOUSLY BENT STEMS

Labrador Tea

Ledum groenlandicum

Other Names

Hudson's Bay tea
Swamp tea
Bog tea

Habitat

This untidy-looking shrub, often growing in large tangled patches, has a strong liking for cold, spongy bogs and muskeg swamps.

WARNING: Be careful not to confuse this species of Labrador tea with another that grows in dry montane areas and that has a bitter taste. Swamp laurel can also be mistaken for Labrador tea. Both swamp laurel and the montane species are toxic, but neither has the rusty, woolly underside to its leaves: be sure to check before picking.

Season

Labrador tea is an evergreen shrub, so the leaves are available for picking all through the year. Opinions differ as to the best time for harvesting. Some people gather the young, upright leaves of spring; others prefer to use the more mature leaves and pick only from October to April, before the plant flowers. During that time, the leaves are reddish-brown and point downwards on the stem.

Preparation

There are at least three ways of preparing tea from this plant. One is to crush a good handful of well-dried leaves and add to four cups of boiling water, then simmer for 5 to 7 minutes. Another way is to put the same amount of dried leaves into four cups of cold water, bring to the boil and simmer for considerably longer, according to taste. This is the kind of tea you can keep on the back of the stove or by the campfire, ready for serving anytime. The third way is to steep the dried flowers, using the same measurements, for 10 minutes or longer to make a delicate and fragrant tea.

WARNING: an excess of Labrador tea could cause drowsiness.

Did you know...

The Inuit and First Nations of eastern Canada used this plant for tea extensively, as did the early explorers, trappers and settlers. The immigrants found, too, that the leaves were effective as a moth and insect repellent.

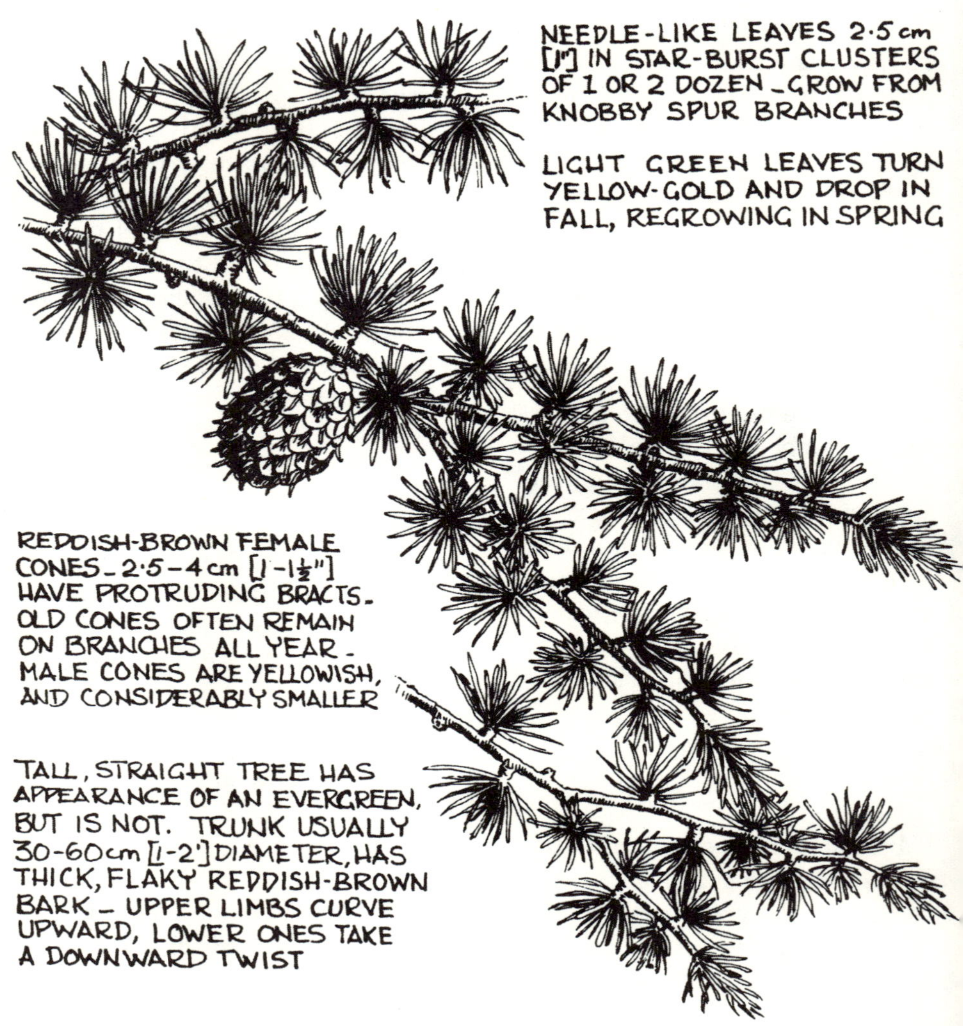

NEEDLE-LIKE LEAVES 2·5 cm
[1"] IN STAR-BURST CLUSTERS
OF 1 OR 2 DOZEN _ GROW FROM
KNOBBY SPUR BRANCHES

LIGHT GREEN LEAVES TURN
YELLOW-GOLD AND DROP IN
FALL, REGROWING IN SPRING

REDDISH-BROWN FEMALE
CONES _ 2·5 - 4 cm [1 - 1½"]
HAVE PROTRUDING BRACTS _
OLD CONES OFTEN REMAIN
ON BRANCHES ALL YEAR _
MALE CONES ARE YELLOWISH,
AND CONSIDERABLY SMALLER

TALL, STRAIGHT TREE HAS
APPEARANCE OF AN EVERGREEN,
BUT IS NOT. TRUNK USUALLY
30-60 cm [1-2'] DIAMETER, HAS
THICK, FLAKY REDDISH-BROWN
BARK _ UPPER LIMBS CURVE
UPWARD, LOWER ONES TAKE
A DOWNWARD TWIST

Western Larch

Larix occidentalis & other species

Other Name

Tamarack

Habitat

The three species of larch are at home in eastern and northern parts of British Columbia south to northeastern Oregon. Two of them prefer mountainous habitats. However, this very attractive conifer is frequently grown as an ornamental tree, so it may often be found beyond its natural bounds.

Season

The leaves, being deciduous, are only available in spring and summer; they can be picked whenever you find them, but are best in late spring.

Preparation

Gather a quantity of the needle-like leaves by picking the knobby spur branches, or pick small twigs. Using them fresh, steep 5 to 10 minutes and savour the resinous and pungent scented tea that results. Add the twigs to a pot of store-bought tea for improved flavour, or use grated cinnamon, cloves and nutmeg, together with dried orange peel, for a spiced tea of high quality.

Did you know...

The heavy wood of larch is valued commercially for its durability and resistance to rotting. It is particularly suitable for railway ties and mineshaft timbers as well as for general construction.

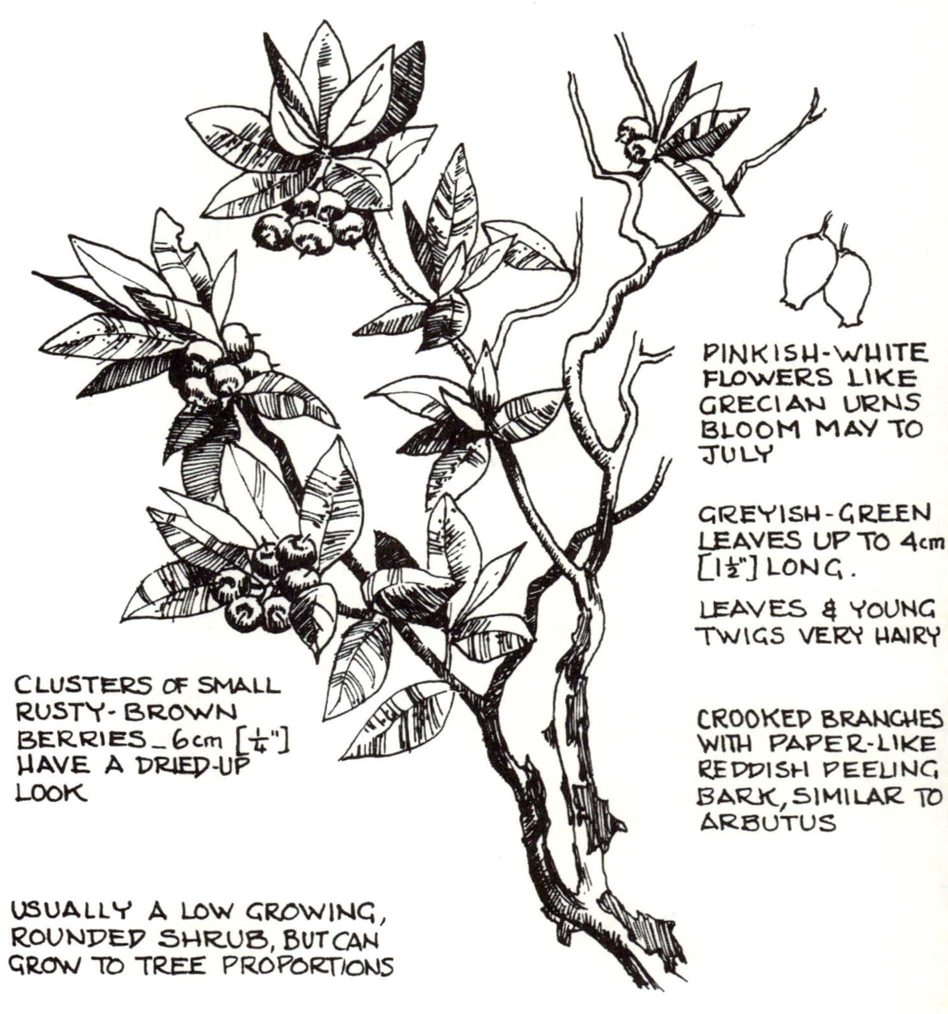

PINKISH-WHITE
FLOWERS LIKE
GRECIAN URNS
BLOOM MAY TO
JULY

GREYISH-GREEN
LEAVES UP TO 4cm
[1½"] LONG.

LEAVES & YOUNG
TWIGS VERY HAIRY

CROOKED BRANCHES
WITH PAPER-LIKE
REDDISH PEELING
BARK, SIMILAR TO
ARBUTUS

CLUSTERS OF SMALL
RUSTY-BROWN
BERRIES _ 6cm [¼"]
HAVE A DRIED-UP
LOOK

USUALLY A LOW GROWING,
ROUNDED SHRUB, BUT CAN
GROW TO TREE PROPORTIONS

Hairy Manzanita

Arctostaphylos columbiana

Habitat

A shrub that chooses dry rocky slopes in full sunshine, this manzanita is limited in range to the Gulf Islands, southern Vancouver Island and the western slopes of the Cascades. Other species range south into California.

Season

The rather unappetizing looking berries ripen in summer and hang on into fall.

Preparation

Wash and clean the berries, scald for a few minutes until they become soft, then crush to a pulp with a potato masher. For each cup of pulp add one cup of water and stir well. Allow the mixture to stand for two hours, then strain and chill. The result is a cool, spicy drink that should not require sweetening.

Did you know...

The name manzanita meaning "small apple" is of Spanish origin—a heritage from the early explorers of the west coast.

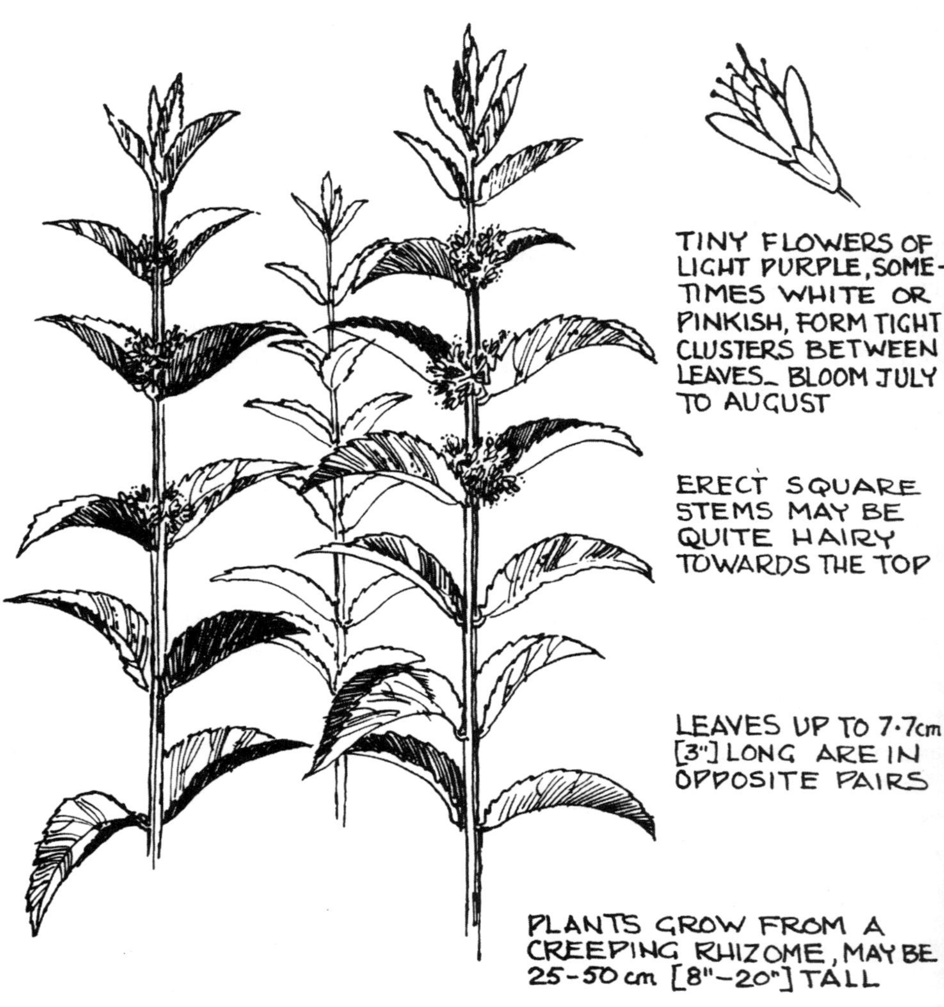

TINY FLOWERS OF
LIGHT PURPLE, SOME-
TIMES WHITE OR
PINKISH, FORM TIGHT
CLUSTERS BETWEEN
LEAVES. BLOOM JULY
TO AUGUST

ERECT SQUARE
STEMS MAY BE
QUITE HAIRY
TOWARDS THE TOP

LEAVES UP TO 7·7cm
[3"] LONG ARE IN
OPPOSITE PAIRS

PLANTS GROW FROM A
CREEPING RHIZOME, MAY BE
25-50 cm [8"-20"] TALL

Wild Mint

Mentha arvensis

Other Names

Canada mint
Swamp mint

Habitat

Mint thrives in moist places such as stream banks and lake shores, and may be found among the long grass of a low-lying meadow. An inconspicuous herb, it is often noticed first by the familiar scent that comes from treading on the plant.

Season

A perennial, mint can be found in spring and summer.

Preparation

Because many cultivated mints have escaped their gardens, there are a number of mint species in the wilds. All can be used for tea, but the one illustrated, a plant native to the west coast, is the best. Crush and steep the fresh leaves—a handful to a medium-sized pot—for 5 to 10 minutes to make a refreshing tea. Or dry the leaves for use at a later date. A heaping teaspoonful per cup should be about right for dried leaves. Try adding cinnamon or dried orange peel, or combine wild mint with your regular tea.

Did you know...

Different species of mint release different perfumed oils when crushed. These may be peppermint, spearmint, apple scented or lemon scented.

MAY GROW AS A TALL SHRUB
OR FULL-SIZED TREE TO 6m [20']

LARGE BUNCHES OF CORAL OR
BRIGHT RED BERRIES BIGGER
THAN PEAS

7 TO 13 LEAFLETS TO EACH
LEAF _ MORE IN SOME
SPECIES _ COARSELY TOOTHED

Mountain Ash

Sorbus scopulina

Other Name

Rowanberry

Habitat

Mountain ash—which is really not an ash at all but a member of the rose family—has several species. Hybridization further complicates exact identification, but locating the plant is no problem. Abundant on mountain slopes, it grows as a shrub with multiple stems; at lower elevations, another species that has a stout trunk and branches grows to tree proportions, and is commonly found at meadow edges and open areas in woods. These trees are descended from ornamental plantings in gardens and along boulevards, their seeds carried into the wild by birds.

Season

The berries ripen in the fall and remain on the branches after the leaves have dropped. Their flavour is improved after they have been touched with frost.

Preparation

For an attractive and refreshing pink lemonade, wash one cup of ripe berries (from any species), mash them and soak the pulp in three cups of cold water for an hour or two. Strain and add sugar to taste. Pour into tall glasses over ice cubes and garnish with a few fresh berries and a small leaf.

You can also use mountain ash berries to make a tasty jelly (see page 130).

Did you know...

Migrating birds often stop on their long journeys to consume large quantities of mountain ash berries.

Some peoples of Europe and Asia have traditionally used—and still use—mountain ash berries to make pie filling or wine, as well as jam and jelly.

A SMALL PLANT
10-36 cm. [4"-14"]
HIGH - SMALLER
IN POOR SOIL

FLAT CIRCULAR SEEDS
WITH RED MARGINS
0·3 cm [⅛"] ACROSS -
SEPTEMBER TO OCTOBER

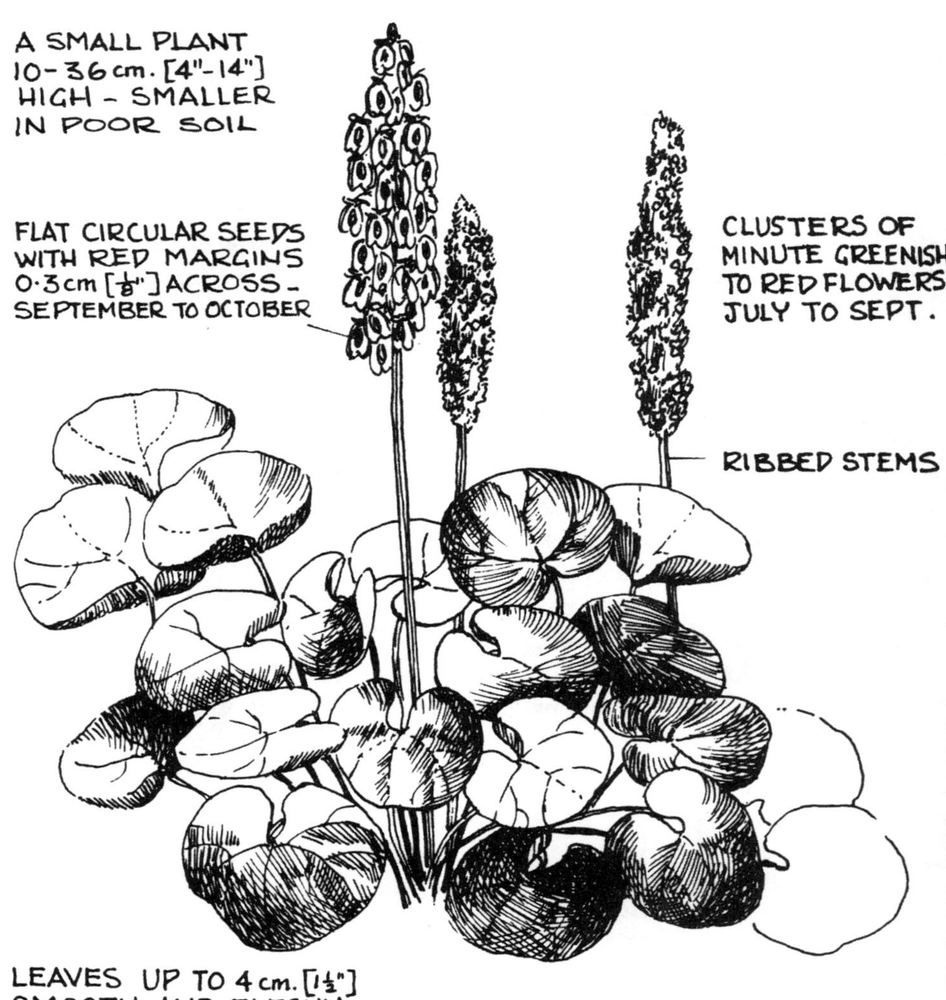

Mountain Sorrel

Oxyria digyna

Other Names

Alpine sorrel
Scurvy grass

Habitat

As its name suggests, this is a plant of the mountains, flourishing up to and above timberline, from Alaska south. Find it in rock crevices and boulder-strewn areas.

Season

Available all summer.

Preparation

The mountain hiker can pause to make a refreshing drink when this plant is available. Finely chop a handful of the fresh leaves, allow them to soak in cold mountain stream water for a while before drinking the lemon flavoured beverage—a sure thirst quencher. Note: So that other hikers may enjoy this sorrel as they pass by, choose to pick the leaves of plants growing away from the trail.

Did you know...

So high in vitamin C is this plant that it was once eaten to prevent scurvy, hence its nickname, scurvy grass. The plant contains oxalic acid but would have to be eaten in great quantities before any harmful effects were felt.

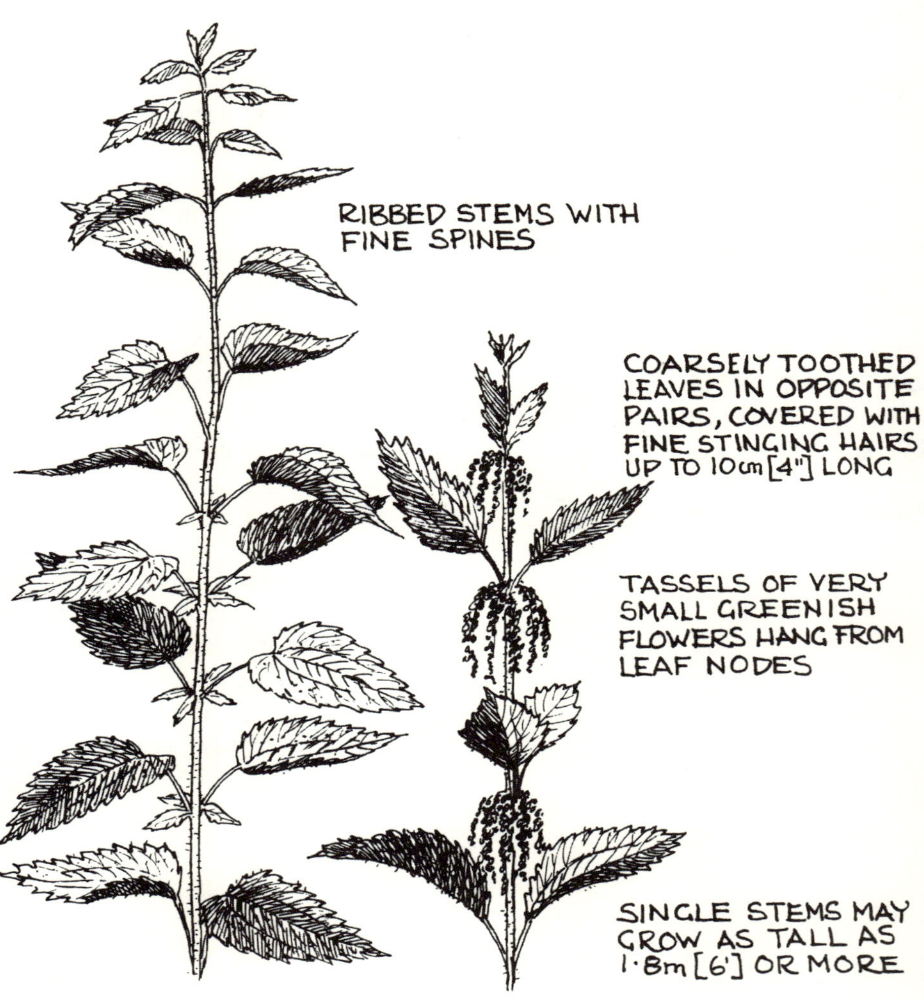

RIBBED STEMS WITH
FINE SPINES

COARSELY TOOTHED
LEAVES IN OPPOSITE
PAIRS, COVERED WITH
FINE STINGING HAIRS
UP TO 10cm [4"] LONG

TASSELS OF VERY
SMALL GREENISH
FLOWERS HANG FROM
LEAF NODES

SINGLE STEMS MAY
GROW AS TALL AS
1·8m [6'] OR MORE

Nettle

Urtica dioica

Other Names

Stinging nettle
Indian spinach

Habitat

Nettle thrives in the rich moist soils
of shaded fields, at forest edges or in
clearings, and along streams and
damp roadsides or pathways.

Season

The young shoots spring up in early
April, and the leaves can be collected
then and throughout the summer.

Preparation

Fresh nettle leaves can cause painful
stinging and itching through contact
with the skin, so be sure to wear
gloves when collecting them. (Plastic
bags slipped over the hands, with the
edges tucked up inside shirt or jacket
cuffs—or held in place with rubber
bands at the wrist—are a good
substitute for gloves.) Once dried,
the leaves lose their sting.

To make a light green herb tea, use
two teaspoons of dried, crumbled
nettle leaves per cup of boiling water,
and steep for 5 to 10 minutes. Add a
sweetener to taste. Try combining it
with mint or pineapple weed.

In spring, young nettles a few inches
high provide a tasty, nutritional pot
herb. Pick the bushy tops (wearing
gloves), and gather plenty, as they
boil down. Rinse well, then drop
into boiling salted water for just a
few minutes. Drain well and add
butter, salt and pepper.

Did you know…

Tall nettle stems were gathered in
the fall by many First Nations
peoples, especially those on the
Pacific coast. Women spun the strong
silky fibres from them into twine for
fish netting and fishing lines, or for
weaving into tump lines, bags and
other items of daily living. In early
times, Europeans also made fishnets
from the fibres, and in fact the word
"net" comes from the word "nettle."

In October, when the plants are tall
and dying down, gather the stalks
and peel back the tough dried outer
"skin." Craftspeople find this strong
nettle twine has many uses. Soak the
fibres in water before working with
them.

GRAPE-LIKE BUNCHES OF
BERRIES_GREEN WHEN
UNRIPE BUT DARK BLUE
WITH LIGHT BLOOM WHEN
RIPE

SPRAYS OF EVERGREEN LEAVES
WITH 11 TO 17 PRICKLY LEAFLET
RISE FROM A WOODY STEM
PLANT ABOUT 60 cm [2'] HIGH

SPIKES 10cm [4"] LONG OF
SMALL YELLOW FLOWERS
BLOOM IN SPRING

Oregon Grape

Mahonia nervosa *or* Berberis nervosa

Other Name

Barberry

Habitat

This shrub is familiar to those who enjoy the coniferous forests west of the Cascade Mountains from southern British Columbia to California, where it often appears in large patches. Oregon grape will produce flowers and fruit only where sufficient light penetrates the forest; otherwise, it remains barren. A similar but taller species of the shrub inhabits open, dry, rocky areas.

Season

Late fall is the best time to gather the grape-like fruits which, because of their colour, many people presume are poisonous. If frost has touched the berries, so much the better.

Preparation

Gather a quantity of berries, rinse them clean and put into a saucepan with just enough water to start the simmer process, then cover. As the fruit breaks up, crush with a potato masher, then strain through a jelly bag. Reheat the resulting liquid and stir in sugar or honey until pleasantly tart but palatable. (Oregon grape is very sour without a sweetener.) Allow to cool, store in the refrigerator and use as a cordial concentrate for a refreshing drink. For a real thirst quencher, mix the juice half and half with ginger ale and pour over crushed ice.

Oregon grapes can also be made into a beautifully coloured and flavourful jelly (see page 131).

Did you know...

The inner bark of the root and stem of Oregon grape is a brilliant yellow and can be used to make fabric dye.

NEEDLES SLENDER, IN PAIRS .
4 - 6.5 cm [1½"- 2½" LONG]
BARK MOTTLED GREY .
SMALL, LOOSE SCALES
CONE HARD, SPINY .
USUALLY CLUSTERED,
MAY HANG ON TREE
UNOPENED FOR YEARS
YOUNG TREES NARROWLY
CONICAL, WITH WHORLS OF
BUSHY UP-TURNED BRANCHES .
HEIGHT OF OLD TREES TO 30m [100']

Pine

Pinus contorta latifolia & other species

Other Names

Jack pine
Scrub pine
Shore pine

Habitat

Although the lodgepole pine is
illustrated here, all species of pine
make a good tea. This means it is
widely available right across the
country.

Preparation

From the pine branches, gather
several twigs with bushy needles at
the tips. The younger growth of
spring is best, but any time of year
is good.

Strip off the needles and, using a
good handful of these to a three-cup
pot, add boiling water and steep ten
minutes. For a single cup use a
generous pinch of needles. The
resulting tea has a delightfully
resinous flavour and is good
combined with store-bought tea, or
with spices. Try adding nutmeg,
cinnamon, or cloves with grated
orange peel, or experiment by mixing
it with other wild teas.

Did you know...

Nature makes special provision for
reforestation of lodgepole pine after
a forest fire. The hard cones, many
of which remain closed on the
branches for several years, resist
burning. After being heated by fire,
they open to release their seeds for
germination.

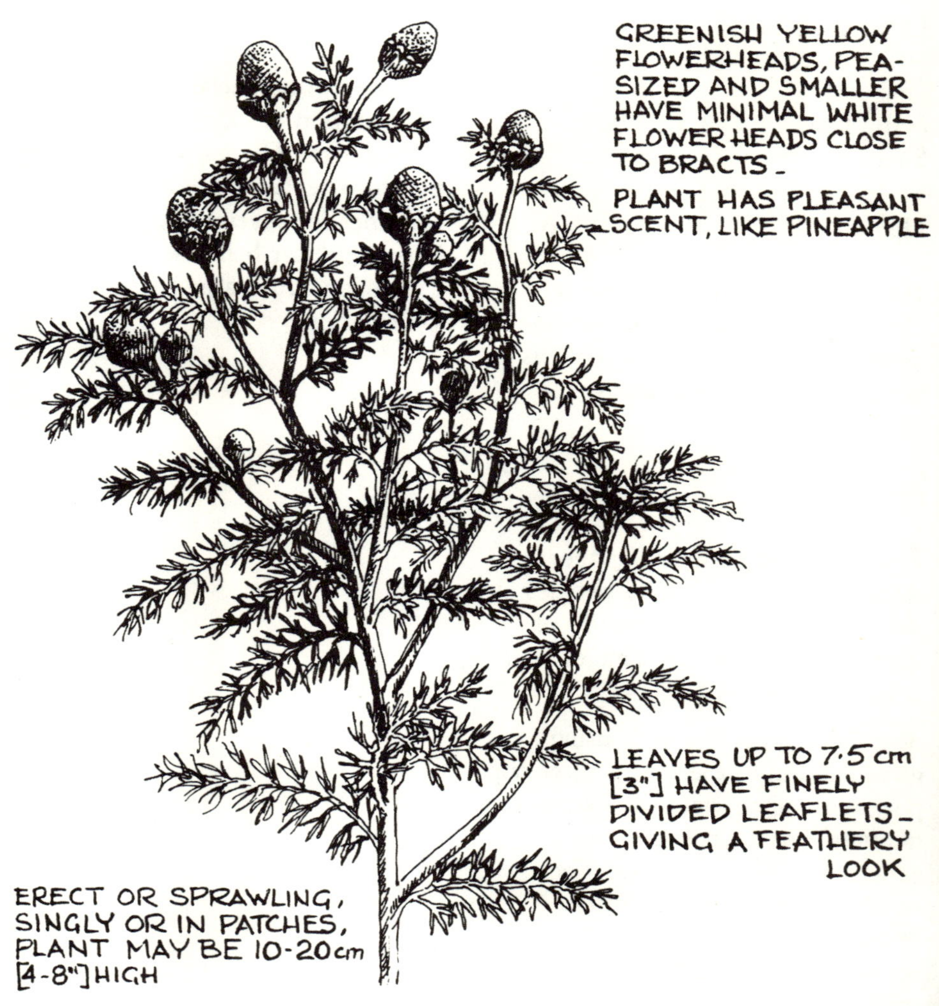

GREENISH YELLOW
FLOWERHEADS, PEA-
SIZED AND SMALLER
HAVE MINIMAL WHITE
FLOWER HEADS CLOSE
TO BRACTS.

PLANT HAS PLEASANT
SCENT, LIKE PINEAPPLE

LEAVES UP TO 7.5 cm
[3"] HAVE FINELY
DIVIDED LEAFLETS_
GIVING A FEATHERY
LOOK

ERECT OR SPRAWLING,
SINGLY OR IN PATCHES,
PLANT MAY BE 10-20 cm
[4-8"] HIGH

Pineapple Weed

Matricaria matricarioides

Habitat

Wherever poor, gravelly soil is hard packed, pineapple weed somehow persists in taking a stand. It thrives in sunny places along pathways and driveways, road edges and even between the cracks of sidewalks or in gravel parking lots.

Season

Flowers appear on the plant in June and continue to blossom until September.

Preparation

The aromatic flower heads dry quickly in a warm place. When dried, add a heaping teaspoon of them to one quart of boiling water and steep in the usual way to make an aromatic tea. The leaves are also strongly scented, but most people find their flavour disagreeable; thus, the use of the flowers only is advisable.

Did you know...

Kootenay First Nation children once strung together the rounded flower heads of this plant for necklaces. Their parents stuffed pillows with the pleasantly scented herb, in addition to using the whole plant to keep insects from food.

For use as beads, pick tight, oval flower heads. Use a needle and strong thread to string them together at the stalk end. The flowers will dry in a few days of warmth, and the wearer will enjoy the pleasant pineapple scent. Or add the flower heads to a bowl of potpourri.

3 TO 9 WAXY FLOWERS,
WHITE TO PINK, CLUSTER
AT TOP OF STEM, BLOOM
IN MAY OR JUNE

LEATHERY, SHARPLY TOOTHED
LEAVES 2·5–5 cm [1–2"] LONG
FORM LOOSE WHORLS AROUND
THE STEM, ARE YELLOW-GREEN
ON UNDERSIDE

LOW PLANT GROWING
12·5–25 cm [5–10"] HIGH

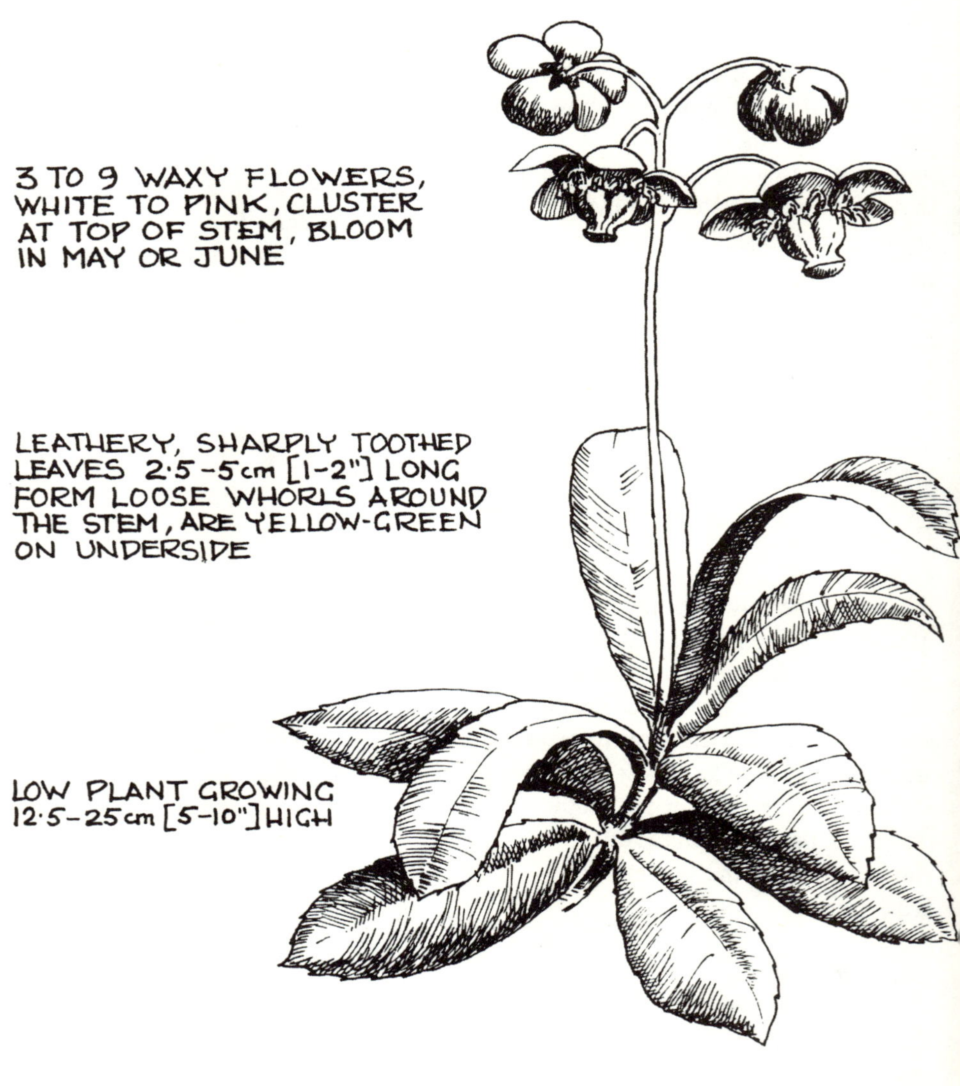

Pipsissewa
Chimaphila umbellata

Other Name

Prince's pine

Habitat

An attractive plant with an unusual name, pipsissewa enjoys the shade and moisture of cool evergreen forests and is often found along stream banks. It may also grow on drier, shrubby slopes but in less abundance.

Season

Pipsissewa is an evergreen and can be found all year round.

Preparation

Both the dried leaves and roots of this charming plant can be boiled, and the liquid cooled to make a refreshing drink. However, because of its uncommon beauty, choose to utilize the leaves rather than the roots, and only when the plant is plentiful. Boil the dried leaves for only a few minutes; overcooking will make the drink bitter.

Did you know...

The leaves of cultured pipsissewa are used as an astringent in the manufacture of modern medicines, and some root beers are flavoured with this plant.

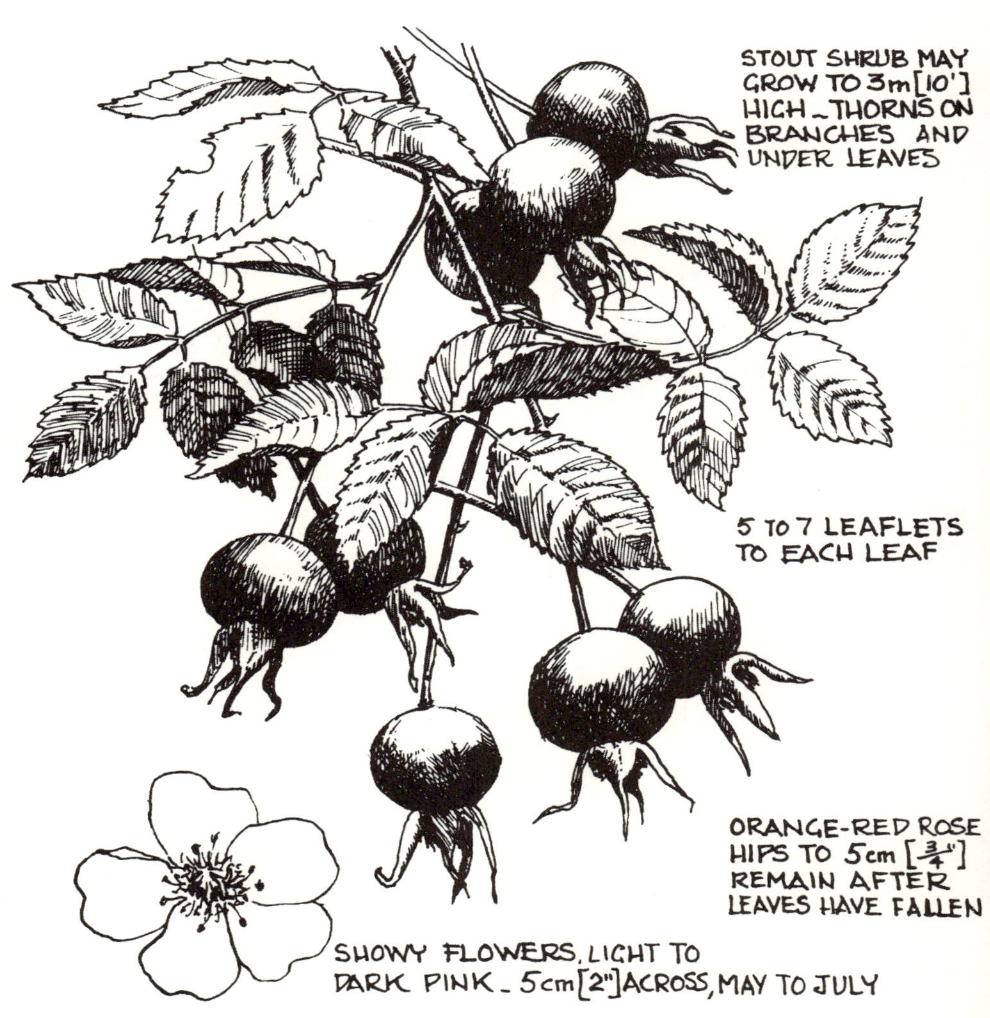

STOUT SHRUB MAY GROW TO 3m [10'] HIGH - THORNS ON BRANCHES AND UNDER LEAVES
5 TO 7 LEAFLETS TO EACH LEAF
ORANGE-RED ROSE HIPS TO 5cm [¾"] REMAIN AFTER LEAVES HAVE FALLEN
SHOWY FLOWERS, LIGHT TO DARK PINK - 5cm [2"] ACROSS, MAY TO JULY

Rose

Rosa nutkana

Other Names

Wild rose
Nootka rose

Habitat

More than 100 species of rose are native to the northern hemisphere. This species of wild rose is a colourful shrub that often grows in gay profusion throughout the West at lower elevations. It prefers rich, moist soil, thriving in open woods, at meadow edges, along country lanes and often at water's edge.

Season

Rose hips (the seeds) remain on the branches throughout most of the winter, but they are at their sweetest after the first frost.

Preparation

For best results, collect rose hips at their prime, around October. Wash them well and remove stems and dried sepals from the ends. The seeds inside are covered with fine, silvery hairs which can cause digestive problems if ingested, so it is better to cut the hips in half and scrape them clean. Crush the fruit and steep for 15 to 20 minutes for a truly delicious drink that will rival any herb tea from the health food store. An alternative to removing the seeds is to strain the tea through a fine cloth.

For successful storage, the halved, cleaned hips must be dried thoroughly, until the flesh is hard and crisp.

The versatile rose hip is also good when finely ground and added to other wild teas. Try it with fireweed, strawberry leaves and pineapple weed for extra flavour.

The scented flowers, fresh or dried, make a fragrant and deliciously flavoured tea, but the quantity required is destructive of this attractive wayside shrub: half a cup of petals is needed for one cup of tea. Better just to use the hips or, for flower-tea, to experiment with the many-petalled garden variety of the plant. The uncoloured base of the petals is bitter and should not be included.

Did you know...

Rose hips contain iron, calcium and phosphorous and are richer than oranges in vitamin C. During the Second World War, the British gathered huge quantities of the hips to replace the citrus fruit that could not be imported.

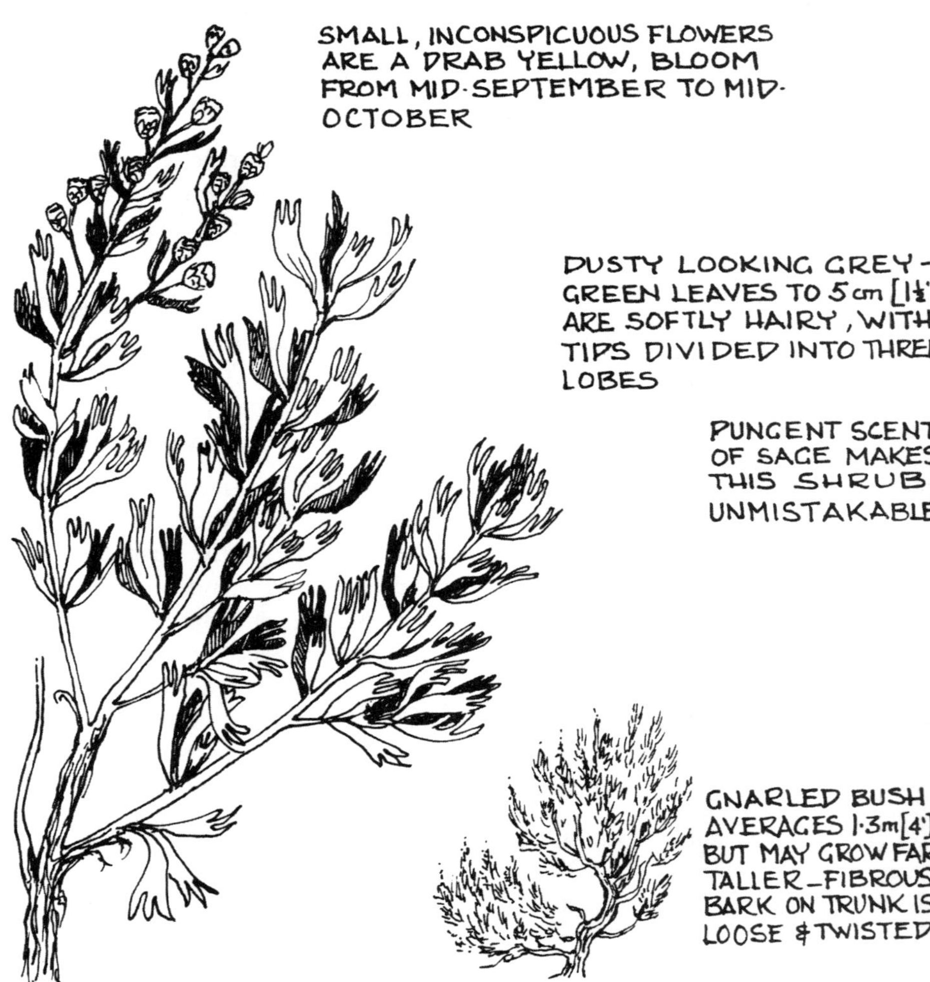

SMALL, INCONSPICUOUS FLOWERS
ARE A DRAB YELLOW, BLOOM
FROM MID·SEPTEMBER TO MID·
OCTOBER

DUSTY LOOKING GREY-
GREEN LEAVES TO 5cm [1½"]
ARE SOFTLY HAIRY, WITH
TIPS DIVIDED INTO THREE
LOBES

PUNGENT SCENT
OF SAGE MAKES
THIS SHRUB
UNMISTAKABLE

GNARLED BUSH
AVERAGES 1·3m[4']
BUT MAY GROW FAR
TALLER—FIBROUS
BARK ON TRUNK IS
LOOSE & TWISTED

Sagebrush

Artemisia tridentata

Habitat

In poor soil throughout the barren areas of the dry interior of British Columbia and eastern Washington, this species of sagebrush thrives in large masses, scenting the air with its pungent aroma.

Season

The soft, grey-green leaves of sage remain on the shrub year round, making this tea available at any time. But, as with many wild teas, the young leaves make the best brew.

Preparation

Pick fresh young leaves from the tips of branches, wash them thoroughly to remove all dust and dry them well in the usual manner. Use a heaping teaspoonful of dried leaves for each cup of boiling water and steep for 15 minutes or longer.

Dried and crumbled, sagebrush can be stored and used in cooking the same way as garden sage. Remove any stalks.

Did you know...

Sagebrush almost always chooses to grow on soils of volcanic origin, rather than on those made from metamorphic rock. The oil from the foliage of several species of this shrub is used in the manufacture of absinthe.

With its pungent scent, sagebrush can be used as a pleasant air freshener. Dry the leaves and allow them to smoulder on the hot top of a wood stove, or simply burn them on a pie plate over a medium hot burner. Try hanging up a bunch of this aromatic herb in your tent, cabin or home, just for the delight of it.

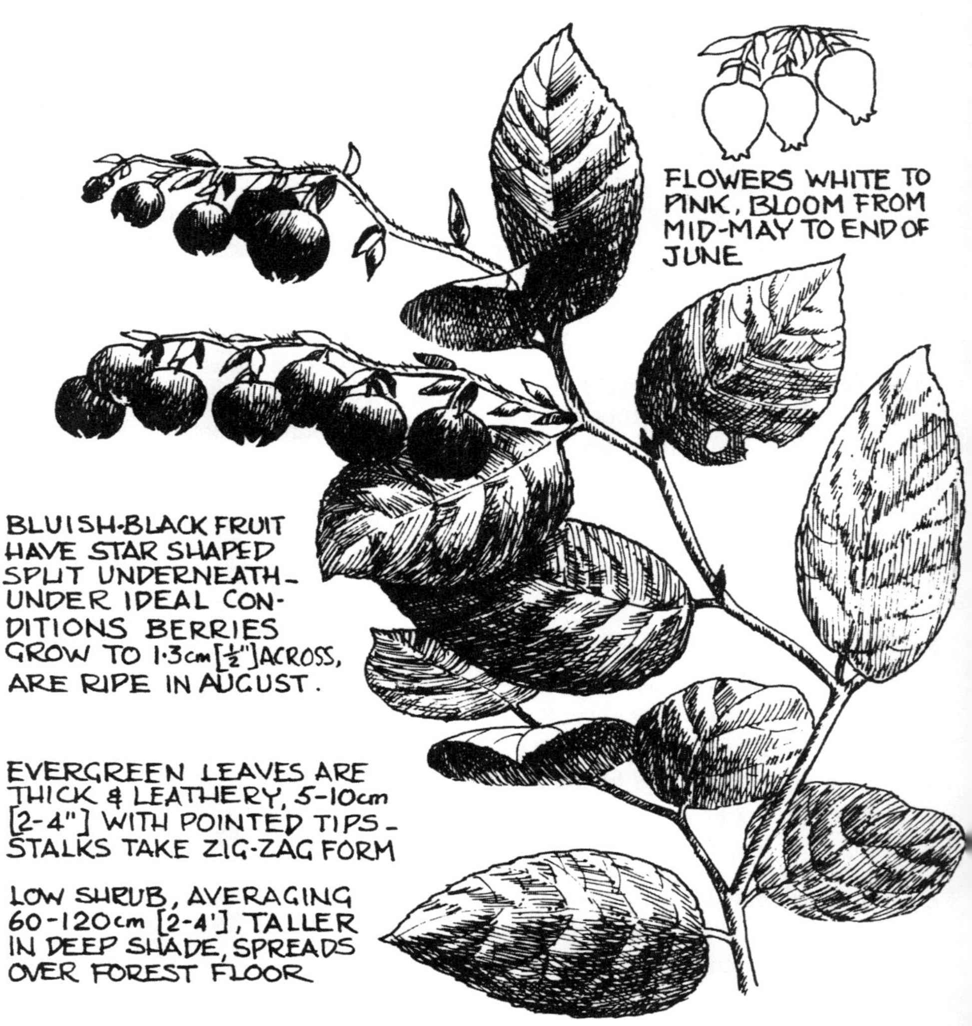

FLOWERS WHITE TO PINK, BLOOM FROM MID-MAY TO END OF JUNE

BLUISH-BLACK FRUIT HAVE STAR SHAPED SPLIT UNDERNEATH - UNDER IDEAL CON- DITIONS BERRIES GROW TO 1·3cm [½"] ACROSS, ARE RIPE IN AUGUST.

EVERGREEN LEAVES ARE THICK & LEATHERY, 5-10cm [2-4"] WITH POINTED TIPS - STALKS TAKE ZIG-ZAG FORM

LOW SHRUB, AVERAGING 60-120cm [2-4'], TALLER IN DEEP SHADE, SPREADS OVER FOREST FLOOR

Salal

Gaultheria shallon

Habitat

Salal is an abundant shrub that favours moist, coastal forests, logged-off areas and open roadsides in rural areas—places where good light is available. The best conditions for a bumper crop of berries are a wet spring and a hot spell in summer.

Season

Salal berries are generally ripe by late June and through July to early August—the sunnier the location, the bigger and better the fruit. Late pickers may find tiny but harmless white caterpillars.

Preparation

Many people think salal berries are poisonous, but they are juicy and delicious. To speed picking, nip off entire stalks of berries and separate them when you get home.

Collect only fully ripe berries and rinse well in cold water, discarding small stems and sepals. Measure and place in a saucepan, adding 1/4 cup water for each 2 cups of berries. Simmer until the fruit breaks up and crush well with a potato masher. Put the pulp in a jelly bag or fine-mesh

sieve and press out the liquid. Sweeten the juice to taste and chill for a delightful drink. Add a drop of vanilla extract for a gourmet touch. The juice may temporarily stain your tongue and teeth. Salal berries also make a delicious jam or jelly (see pages 131 and 132).

Did you know…

On the Pacific coast, First Nations women gathered, crushed and dried large quantities of salal berries to eat in the winter. To brighten up outdoor plant tubs and large pots in the winter, "plant" large sprays of the evergreen salal leaves, which will last for a long time in wet soil. This won't harm the shrubs that you cut the sprays from, as salal readily grows new branches where cut.

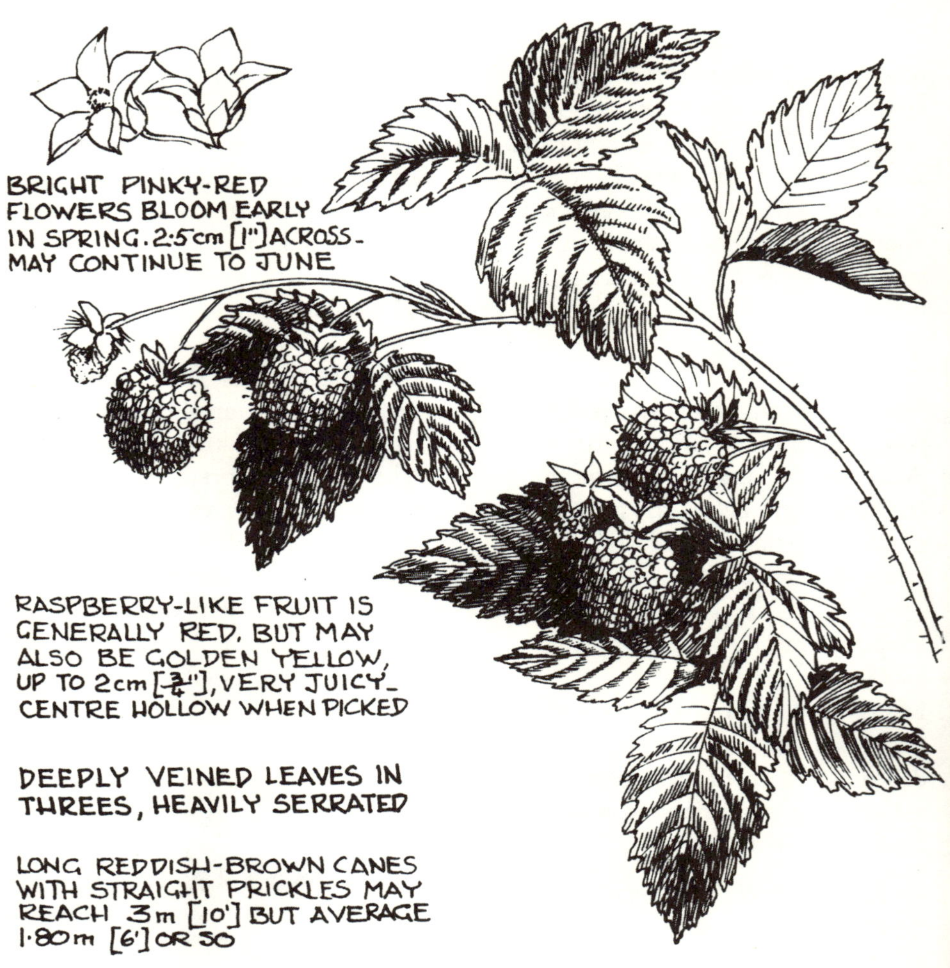

BRIGHT PINKY-RED
FLOWERS BLOOM EARLY
IN SPRING. 2·5 cm [1"] ACROSS.
MAY CONTINUE TO JUNE

RASPBERRY-LIKE FRUIT IS
GENERALLY RED, BUT MAY
ALSO BE GOLDEN YELLOW,
UP TO 2 cm [¾"], VERY JUICY.
CENTRE HOLLOW WHEN PICKED

DEEPLY VEINED LEAVES IN
THREES, HEAVILY SERRATED

LONG REDDISH-BROWN CANES
WITH STRAIGHT PRICKLES MAY
REACH 3 m [10'] BUT AVERAGE
1·80 m [6'] OR SO

Salmonberry

Rubus spectabilis

Habitat

Often forming large clumps or extensive thickets, salmonberry flourishes on the Pacific coast in moist, shady places, along creeks and roadsides and on the shaded sides of clearings and meadows.

Season

Salmonberries are the first berries of the year, ripening as early as May in sheltered areas and continuing into late June.

Preparation

These juicy berries can range in flavour from delicious to bland. Gather three quarters of a cup of berries, crush them, and add cold water to fill the cup. Stir in a teaspoonful of sugar and a dash of vanilla or almond extract, then pour over crushed ice in a tall glass.

Alternatively, crush the salmonberries and stir them into melted ice cream mixed with half milk. (Children like it!)

Did you know...

On the Pacific coast, salmonberries were widely used by First Nations peoples, who also relished eating the sweet, succulent young shoots after peeling off the outer skin and prickles. Families or chiefs often owned the right to certain berry patches, giving them the privilege of first (and best) picking.

Some Kwakwaka'wakw First Nations men made arrow shafts from the long, straight stems of the salmonberry bush.

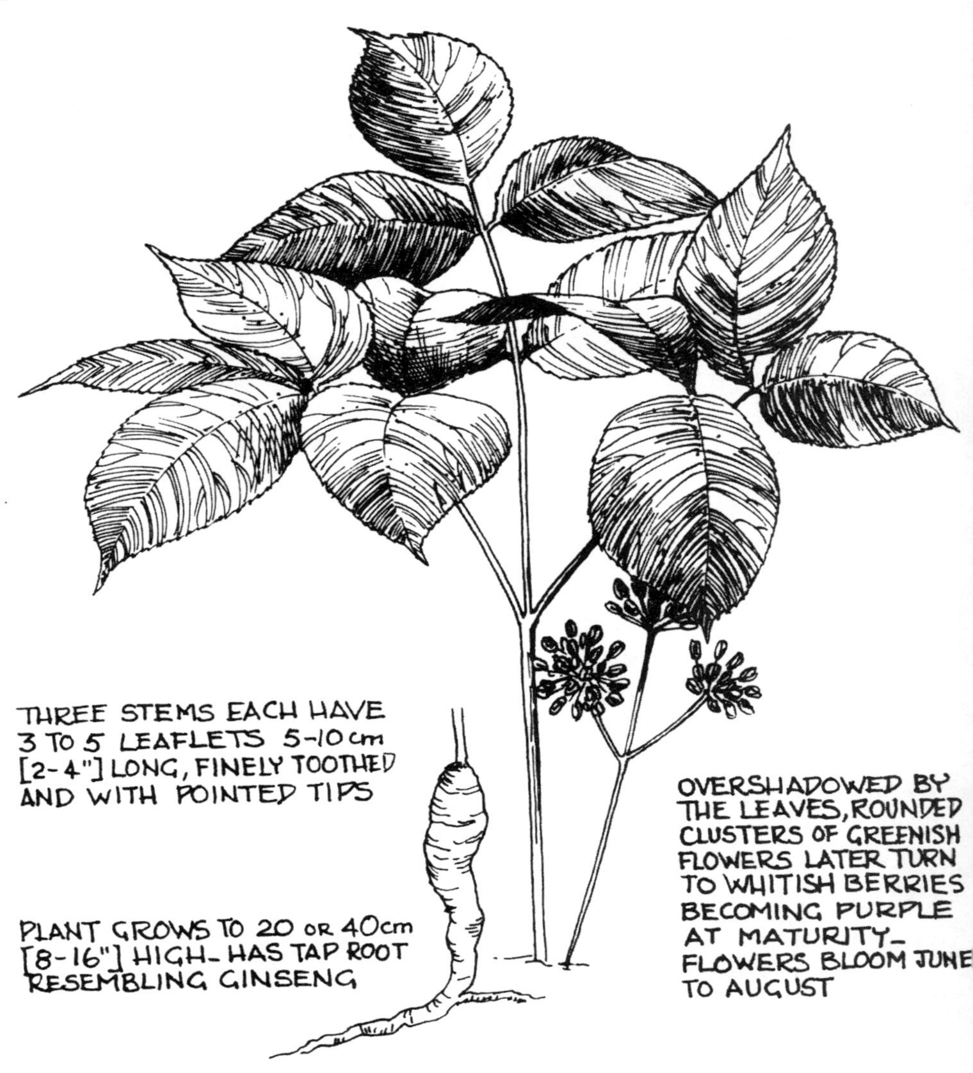

THREE STEMS EACH HAVE
3 TO 5 LEAFLETS 5-10 cm
[2-4"] LONG, FINELY TOOTHED
AND WITH POINTED TIPS

PLANT GROWS TO 20 OR 40cm
[8-16"] HIGH_ HAS TAP ROOT
RESEMBLING GINSENG

OVERSHADOWED BY
THE LEAVES, ROUNDED
CLUSTERS OF GREENISH
FLOWERS LATER TURN
TO WHITISH BERRIES
BECOMING PURPLE
AT MATURITY_
FLOWERS BLOOM JUNE
TO AUGUST

Wild Sarsaparilla
Aralia nudicaulis

Other Names

Wild ginseng
Wild spikenard

Habitat

Although it may grow in large
patches, wild sarsaparilla is often
not recognized. In our area it thrives
in the moist, shaded or semi-open
forests of south-central and
southeastern British Columbia and
northeastern Washington.

Season

The root is at its best before the
plant flowers, and again after an
autumn frost.

Preparation

To make a sarsaparilla-like drink,
gather one or two roots, hang them
in a warm place until well dried,
then pound into a flour. Stir three or
more teaspoons of ground root into
a cup of boiling water, add honey to
taste; cool, then chill for a fragrant,
spicy drink of a reddish-brown
colour. Another method is to chop
the roots and boil them until the
water becomes a reddish colour; add
a sweetener and serve hot.

Did you know...

Sarsaparilla is a drink that enjoyed
great popularity in the late
nineteenth century. Made from
extracts of the roots of a species of
Smilax, an evergreen vine of South
America, it was said to be a good
tonic and a "blood purifier," but
modern analysis can find no
beneficial ingredients in the root.

SQUARISH FLOWER
HEADS COMPRISED OF
ORCHID-LIKE FLOWERS
RANGING FROM PINK OR
PURPLE TO VIOLET AND
BLUE —OCCASIONALLY
WHITE

LEAVES, 2·5 – 6·5 cm
[1"–2½"] GROW IN
OPPOSITE PAIRS

SQUARE STEMS

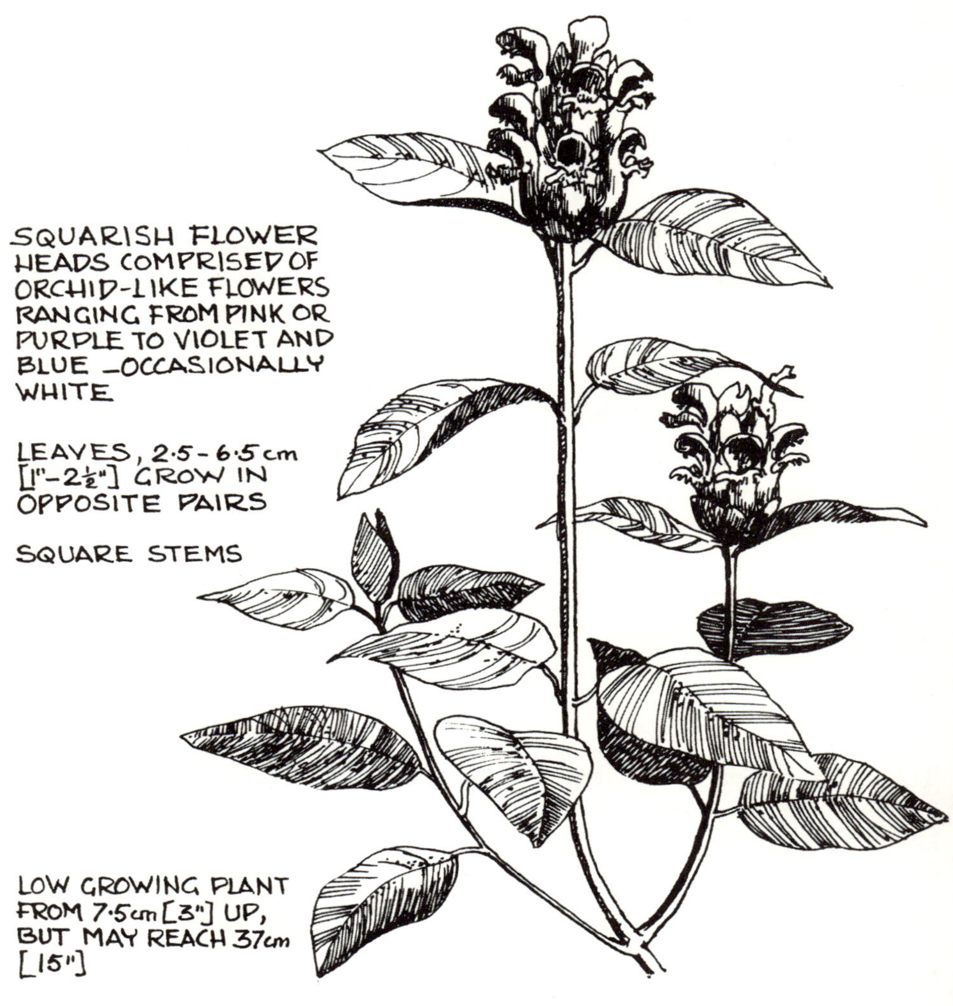

LOW GROWING PLANT
FROM 7·5 cm [3"] UP,
BUT MAY REACH 37 cm
[15"]

Self-heal

Prunella vulgaris

Other Name

Heal-all

Habitat

A common member of the mint family, self-heal is generally found in shaded, moist ground throughout the cool areas of the West.

Season

This perennial continues flowering during the entire summer and can therefore be easily spotted almost anytime.

Preparation

The entire plant may be utilized for a tea, but it is best to gather only the leaves, leaving the plant to continue its growth. Self-heal, either fresh or dried, can be made into a cooling drink. Chop a handful of the green leaves and soak them in two cups of cold water for a good half hour or more, or crush the dried leaves to a powder and mix one heaping teaspoonful to two cups of cold water. Vary the amount to suit your personal taste, and add sugar as required.

Did you know...

As its common names suggest, self-heal was once thought to have curative ingredients for treating several ailments, but modern research can find nothing in the plant to substantiate this claim.

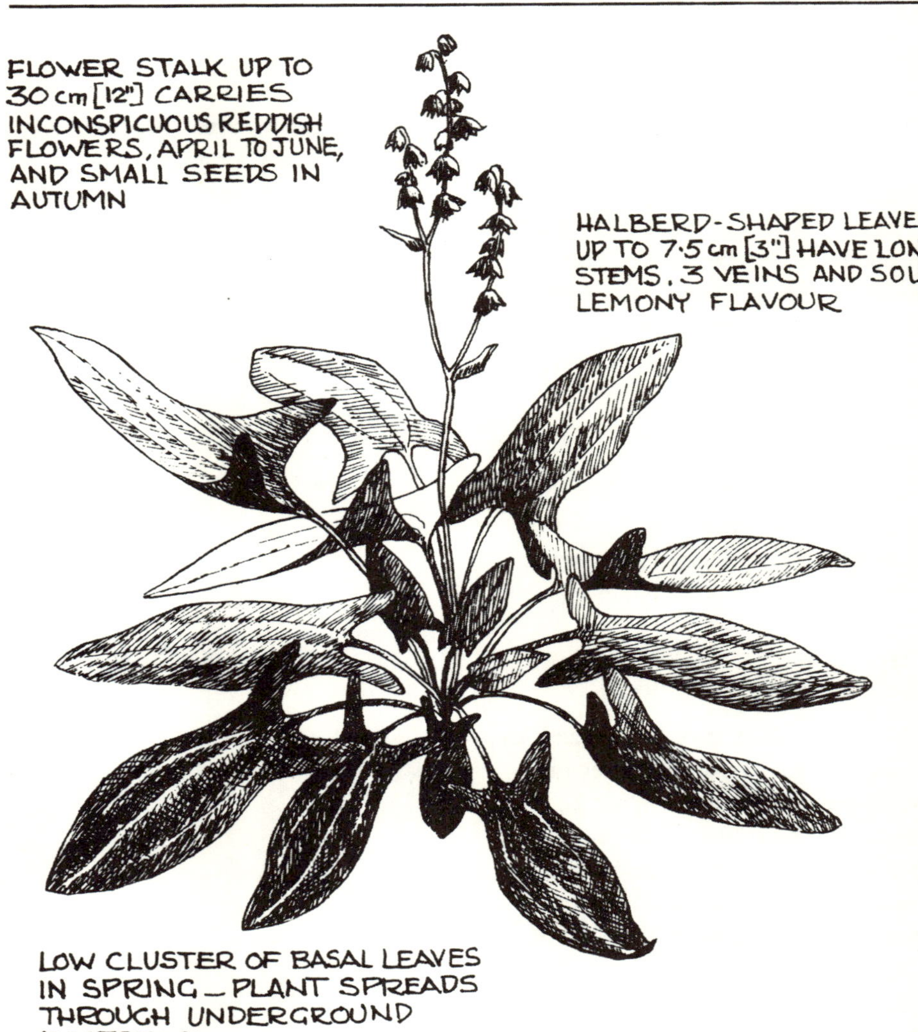

FLOWER STALK UP TO
30 cm [12"] CARRIES
INCONSPICUOUS REDDISH
FLOWERS, APRIL TO JUNE,
AND SMALL SEEDS IN
AUTUMN

HALBERD-SHAPED LEAVES
UP TO 7.5 cm [3"] HAVE LONG
STEMS, 3 VEINS AND SOUR,
LEMONY FLAVOUR

LOW CLUSTER OF BASAL LEAVES
IN SPRING — PLANT SPREADS
THROUGH UNDERGROUND
ROOTSTOCK

Sheep Sorrel
Rumex acetosella

Other Names

Common sorrel
Sourgrass

Habitat

A prolific weed of exposed sandy soils, roadways, gardens and edges of pathways, sheep sorrel can be found almost anywhere from sea level to 1000 metres {3000 feet}. Children know it for the lemon-flavoured leaves they like to nibble, hence the nickname "sourgrass."

Season

Sheep sorrel can be found all year round in mild climates, but the young leaves of spring and summer are the best to use.

Preparation

Here is a dual purpose plant, providing both a hot and a cold drink. To make a tea, dry the leaves in the usual manner, add a good teaspoonful to each cup of water, simmer 20 minutes and strain. Add honey to taste. For lemonade: to five cups of cold water add one-quarter cup finely chopped fresh sorrel leaves, four teaspoons of sumac lemonade (or two teaspoons of lemon juice), one-eighth teaspoon salt, three tablespoons of sugar. Stir well and allow to stand overnight. Strain and pour into a jug with ice cubes; float a few fresh leaves on top.

Did you know...

Gardeners of this continent consider the ubiquitous sorrel an undesirable weed, but in some gardens of Europe it is cultivated as an edible plant.

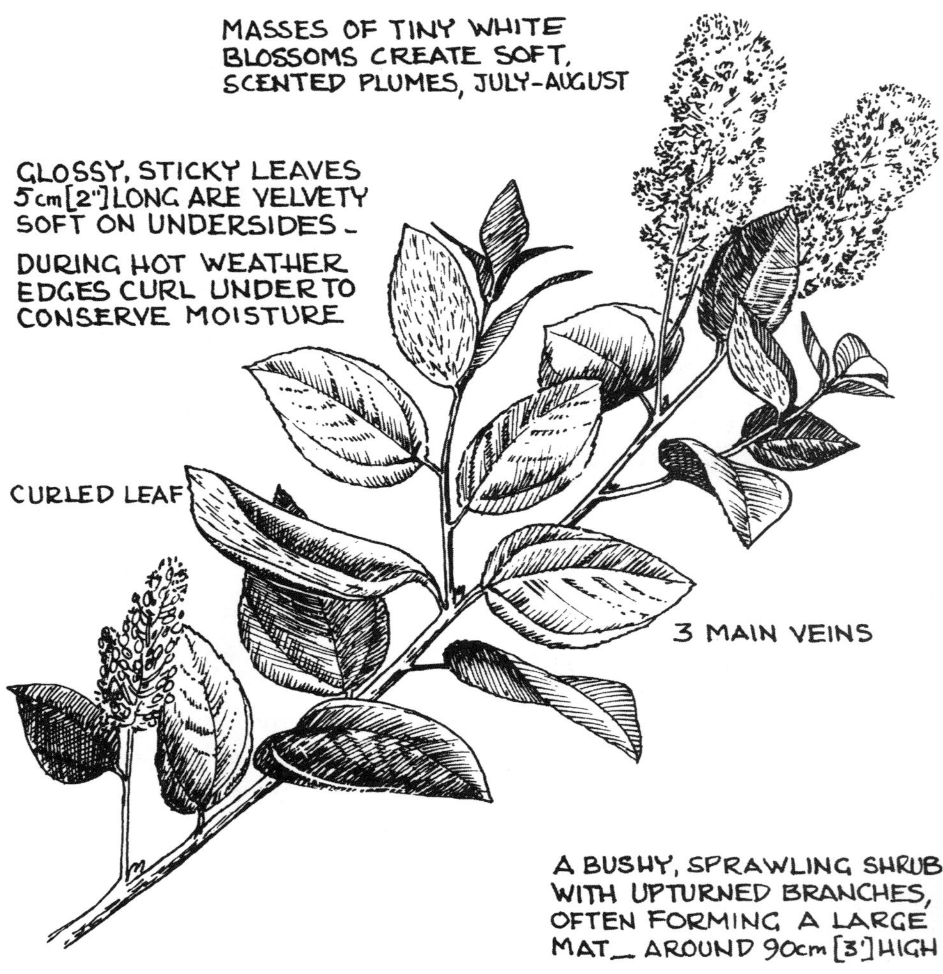

MASSES OF TINY WHITE
BLOSSOMS CREATE SOFT,
SCENTED PLUMES, JULY-AUGUST
GLOSSY, STICKY LEAVES
5cm[2"] LONG ARE VELVETY
SOFT ON UNDERSIDES _
DURING HOT WEATHER
EDGES CURL UNDER TO
CONSERVE MOISTURE
CURLED LEAF
3 MAIN VEINS
A BUSHY, SPRAWLING SHRUB
WITH UPTURNED BRANCHES,
OFTEN FORMING A LARGE
MAT _ AROUND 90cm [3'] HIGH

Snowbrush

Ceanothus velutinus

Other Names

Mountain balm
Sticky laurel
Buckbrush
Wild lilac
Greasewood

Habitat

Snowbrush grows abundantly in poor, gravelly soils, on rocky or semi-barren slopes and flats which offer full sunshine.

Season

This is an evergreen. The leaves are available all year, and flowers blossom in June.

Preparation

To make an excellent drink having the colour and flavour of an Oriental tea, pick the leaves when the flowers are in bloom, and dry thoroughly. The camper or wayfarer, however, can steep the fresh leaves for a reasonably good drink. Finely crumble the dried leaves and use them like store-bought tea, adding a squeeze of lemon if you wish, or a touch of mint.

Alternatively, dry the creamy white flowers, and brew a tasty tea by steeping a heaped teaspoon of these in two cups of boiling water.

Did you know...

The scented blossoms of snowbrush make an excellent soap substitute when dipped in water and rubbed between the hands. The lather produced cleanses the skin and leaves it pleasantly fragrant.

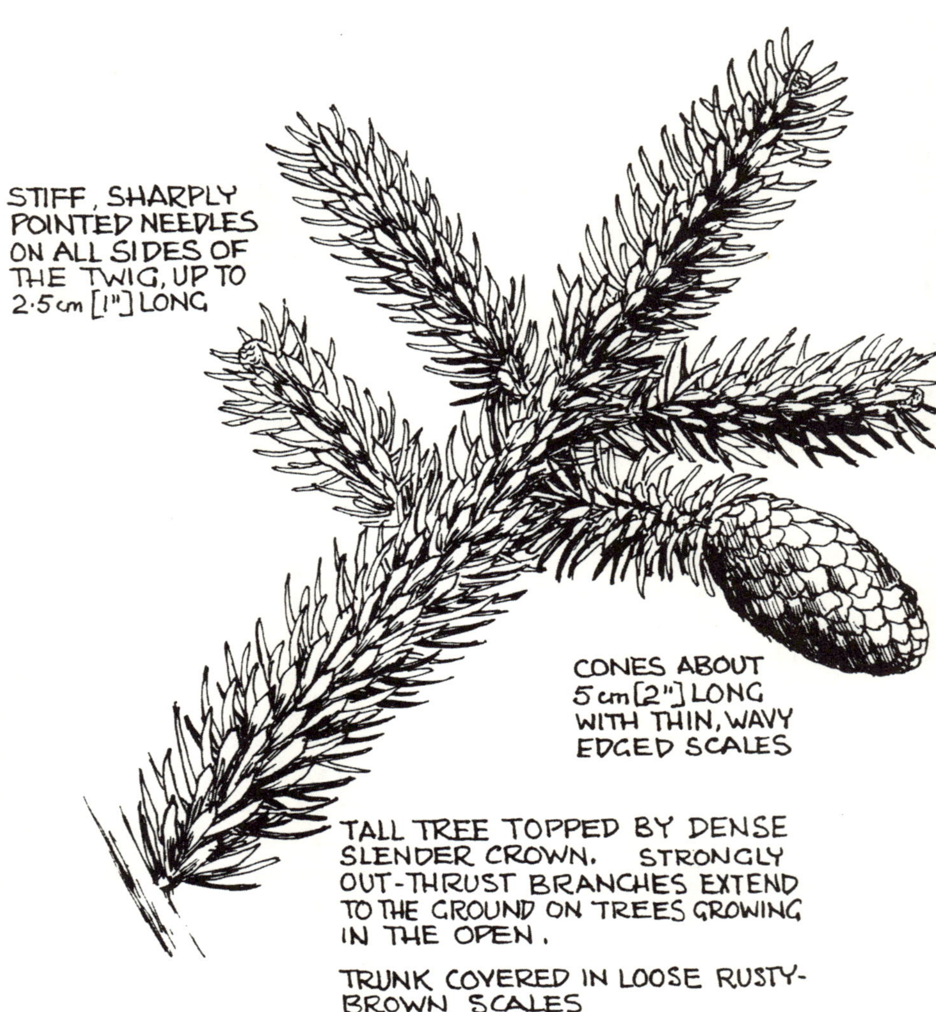

STIFF, SHARPLY
POINTED NEEDLES
ON ALL SIDES OF
THE TWIG, UP TO
2·5 cm [1"] LONG

CONES ABOUT
5 cm [2"] LONG
WITH THIN, WAVY
EDGED SCALES

TALL TREE TOPPED BY DENSE
SLENDER CROWN.   STRONGLY
OUT-THRUST BRANCHES EXTEND
TO THE GROUND ON TREES GROWING
IN THE OPEN.

TRUNK COVERED IN LOOSE RUSTY-
BROWN SCALES

Spruce

Picea sitchensis & other species

Habitat

Thriving on the humidity of rain and fog, the Sitka spruce is particularly abundant on the Queen Charlotte Islands (Haida Gwaii) and the west coast of Vancouver Island. Elsewhere in the Pacific Northwest, it is confined to a wide coastal strip from sea level to around 600 metres (2000 feet).

Other spruces of the West, found in the northern interior of British Columbia or at alpine elevations, are also suitable for use as a tea.

Season

The fresh young needles that grow from the tips of branches in spring make the best tea, but, of course, spruce is an evergreen, so it is available all year round.

Preparation

Gather a handful of spruce needles for each cup of tea. The young needles are soft and easy to handle, but watch out for the sharp spikes on the rest of the branches! You can use the needles either fresh or dried. Steep them in boiling water for a good 10 minutes for a flavourful drink.

Did you know...

During the Second World War, spruce wood was exported from the Queen Charlotte Islands to England for use in the manufacture of light combat aircraft.

Women of both the Haida and Tlingit First Nations of the Queen Charlotte Islands and Alaska made extensive use of spruce roots, splitting them and weaving them into exquisitely fine baskets and decorated hats.

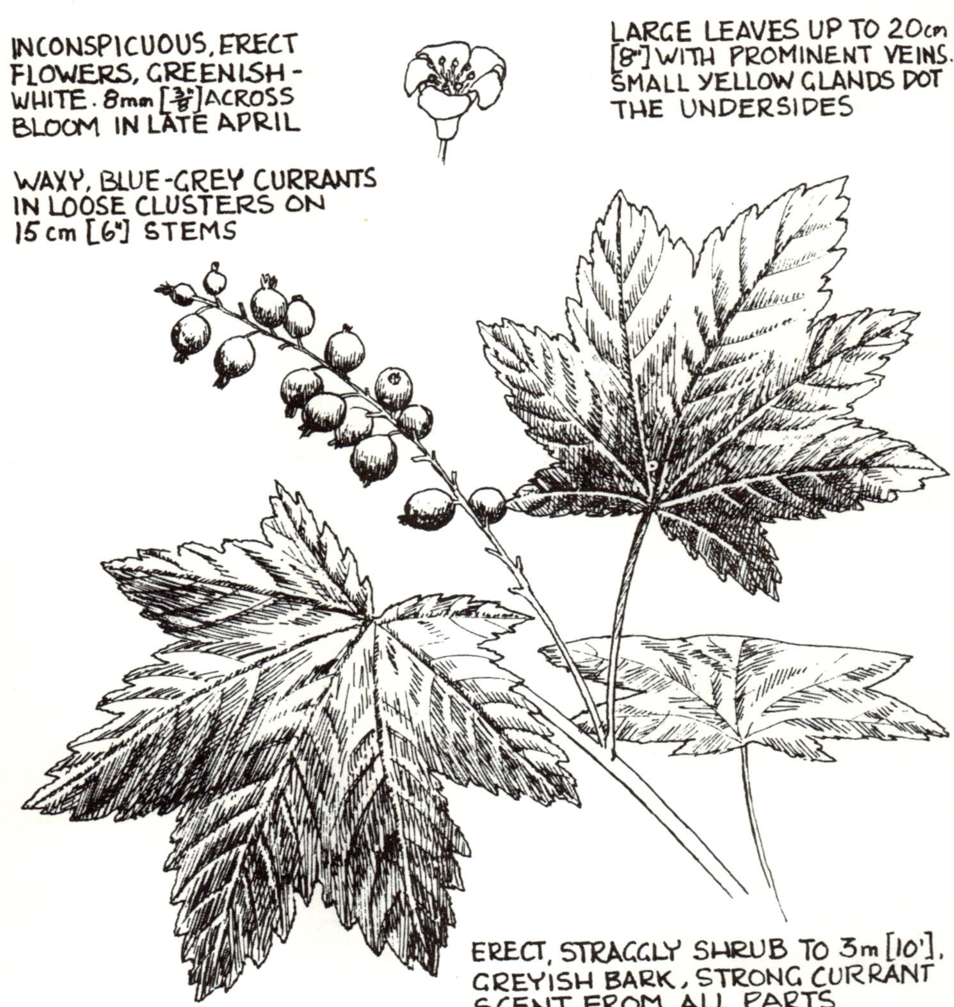

INCONSPICUOUS, ERECT
FLOWERS, GREENISH -
WHITE. 8mm [⅜"] ACROSS
BLOOM IN LATE APRIL

WAXY, BLUE-GREY CURRANTS
IN LOOSE CLUSTERS ON
15 cm [6"] STEMS

LARGE LEAVES UP TO 20cm
[8"] WITH PROMINENT VEINS.
SMALL YELLOW GLANDS DOT
THE UNDERSIDES

ERECT, STRAGGLY SHRUB TO 3m [10'],
GREYISH BARK, STRONG CURRANT
SCENT FROM ALL PARTS

Stink Currant

Ribes bracteosum

Other Names

Blue currant
Greyberry
Skunk currant

Habitat

The strong currant scent may well draw your attention to this tall shrub before you actually see it, but the plant does not deserve its derogatory name, for the aroma is quite pleasant. Look for it in rich black soil beside shaded streams or swampy areas of woodlands, usually west of the Cascade Mountains.

Season

Stink currant puts out fresh new leaves in the spring and loses them in the fall. The berries ripen in late summer.

Preparation

Collect several of the large leaves in spring or later in the year and use them fresh or dried. Use two fresh leaves, crushed (or two heaped teaspoons of dried crumbled leaves) per cup of boiling water and steep for 10 minutes. The result is a tea of palest green, with a delicate currant flavour. You may toss in a few fresh berries to enrich the flavour, or try mixing it with other wilderness teas.

Did you know...

First Nations peoples served these currants in many different ways, both fresh and preserved. The Kwakwaka'wakw picked them fresh and ate them at informal feasts, using spoons made from mountain goat horns. For people of high rank, such as chiefs and their wives, the fruit was mashed with salal berries. The currants were preserved for winter by boiling them with dried, powdered skunk cabbage leaves, forming the mash into cakes, and drying these on frames set over the fire.

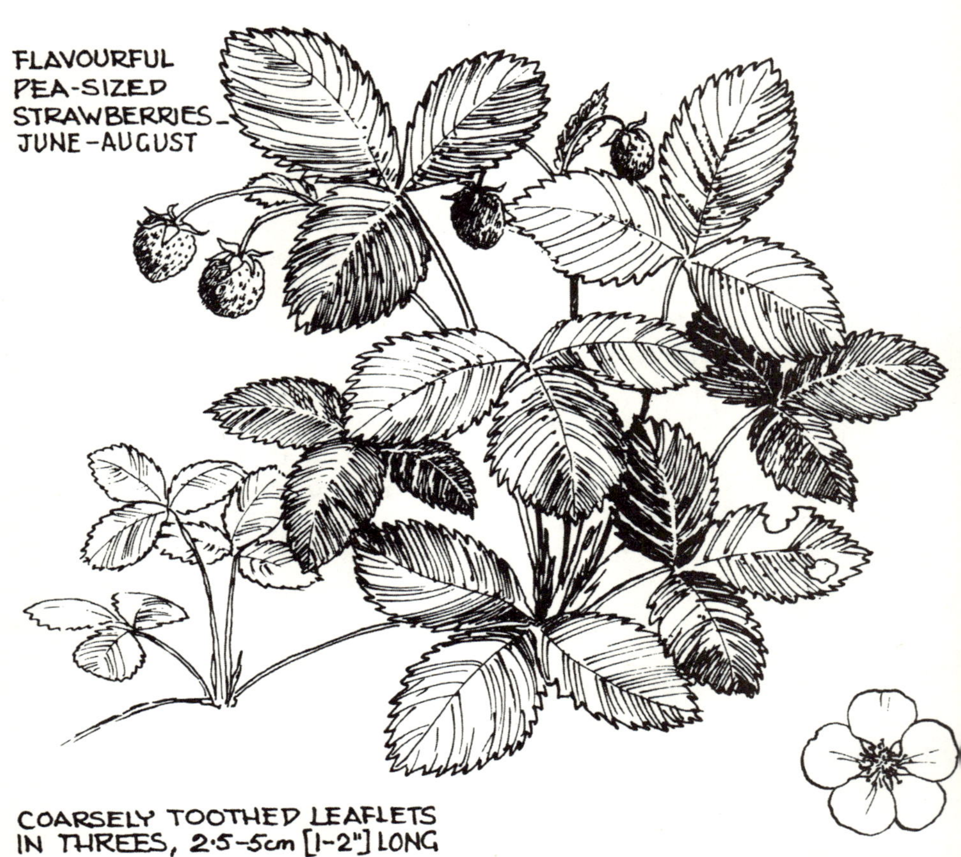

FLAVOURFUL
PEA-SIZED
STRAWBERRIES —
JUNE-AUGUST

COARSELY TOOTHED LEAFLETS
IN THREES, 2·5-5cm [1-2"] LONG

PLANT SPRAWLS CLOSE TO THE
GROUND, SENDS OUT SLENDER
RUNNERS THAT ROOT AND GROW
NEW PLANTS

5-PETALED WHITE
FLOWERS, 1·5cm [⅝"]
ACROSS, WITH
YELLOW CENTRES,
BLOOM IN SPRING

Wild Strawberry

Fragaria virginiana *& other species*

Habitat

Several species of wild strawberry grow right across Canada and the United States. Since all of them have that unmistakable strawberry appearance (though much smaller than commercially sold ones), finding this plant should present no problem. Look for it on well-drained soils in sunny places such as open woodlands, clearings, meadows, rock crevices and hillsides.

Season

Available throughout the summer.

Preparation

Strawberry leaves are rich in vitamin C and make a flavourful, nutritious tea; they can be used fresh or dried. Pick a handful of the fresh mature leaves or use a tablespoon of thoroughly dried, crumbled leaves to make two cups of tea, steeping for about 5 minutes. This is an excellent tea to enjoy on its own for its delicate flavour or to blend with others.

Strawberries themselves also make a refreshing summer drink, hot or cold. Simply crush a tablespoonful or more in a cup and add boiling water, or put the mashed strawberries in a tall glass with cold water and crushed ice, topping it with a leaf sprig.

Wild strawberry jam (see page 132) is also a real treat, redolent of summer.

Berries to spare? Dry them whole, in the sun, to recapture—sometime around the middle of December—the essence of summer. That goes for the dried leaves, too.

Did you know...

All of our cultivated strawberries originate from the wild species. This plant is well known for its antiseptic qualities, and the Okanagan First Nation people used the dried, pulverized leaves to promote healing of the navel of a newborn baby.

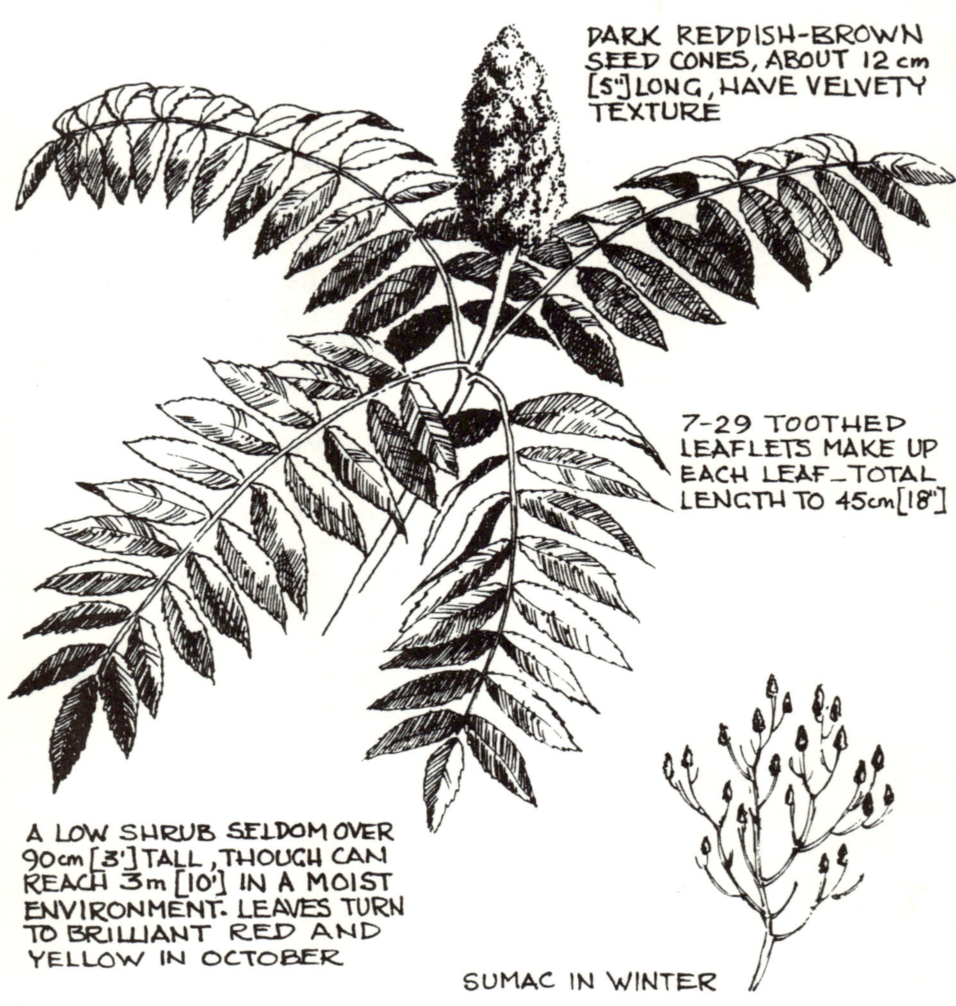

DARK REDDISH-BROWN
SEED CONES, ABOUT 12 cm
[5"] LONG, HAVE VELVETY
TEXTURE

7-29 TOOTHED
LEAFLETS MAKE UP
EACH LEAF - TOTAL
LENGTH TO 45cm [18"]

A LOW SHRUB SELDOM OVER
90cm [3'] TALL, THOUGH CAN
REACH 3m [10'] IN A MOIST
ENVIRONMENT. LEAVES TURN
TO BRILLIANT RED AND
YELLOW IN OCTOBER

SUMAC IN WINTER

Sumac

Rhus glabra

Other Names

Lemonade berry

Habitat

Look for sumac on sunny hillsides at lower elevations in the dry interior regions of British Columbia, southward to Oregon. Because of its ornamental qualities and brilliant autumn colours, another species of sumac (*R. typhina*) can often be found in city gardens, where it may grow to a height of 3 metres (10 feet) or more.

Season

The greenish-yellow fruiting cones of spring give way to deep reddish-brown seed heads by fall. These remain on the branches well into winter but eventually deteriorate with time, so it is best to gather them early.

Preparation

The nickname for this shrub gives away its secret, and just handling the seeds and then licking your fingers will tell you that they have a strong lemon flavour.

Here is all that is required for an excellent "lemonade" with an inviting amber colour: take one seed cone and break apart, then pour a cup of boiling water over it; crush the seeds a little and allow to steep for half an hour. Strain and sweeten with a little honey. Chill before drinking.

Another method is to crush the seed cones in cold water and allow to sit for several hours, preferably overnight, then strain and add sugar. This gives a pink lemonade that is ideal for small children to make, since boiling water is not involved.

Did you know...

People of the Okanagan First Nation predicted the migration of sockeye salmon by watching the sumac. As the leaves turned red, so did the salmon, heralding their return to the lakes to spawn.

SLENDER REDDISH
STEMS CARRY LEAVES
UP TO 5cm [2"] LONG,
COARSELY TOOTHED
ALONG UPPER THIRD
ONLY_ WHITISH TINGE
ON UNDERSIDE

GREEN CATKINS FORM
ON BRANCH TIPS IN
EARLY SPRING, OPEN
LATER TO FORM REDDISH-
BROWN CONE-LIKE
HUSKS

LEAF BUDS —

A MANY-BRANCHED, BUSHY
SHRUB FROM 30 -120 cm
[1-4'] IN HEIGHT

Sweet Gale
Myrica gale

Other Name

Bog Myrtle

Habitat

A water-loving shrub, sweet gale thrives along the fringes of shallow-edged lakes and slow streams as well as in sphagnum bogs of Oregon, Washington, British Columbia, and up the coast to Alaska.

Season

The leaves appear in spring and remain until late fall.

Preparation

To crush a single leaf of sweet gale and sniff the pungent, spicy aroma is to gain a hint of the flavour of this tea. Gather the leaves and dry them in the usual manner, then crush and steep for 10 to 15 minutes to ensure the full piquancy of this drink.

Did you know...

Early pioneers used crushed, dried sweet gale leaves as a seasoning for meat.

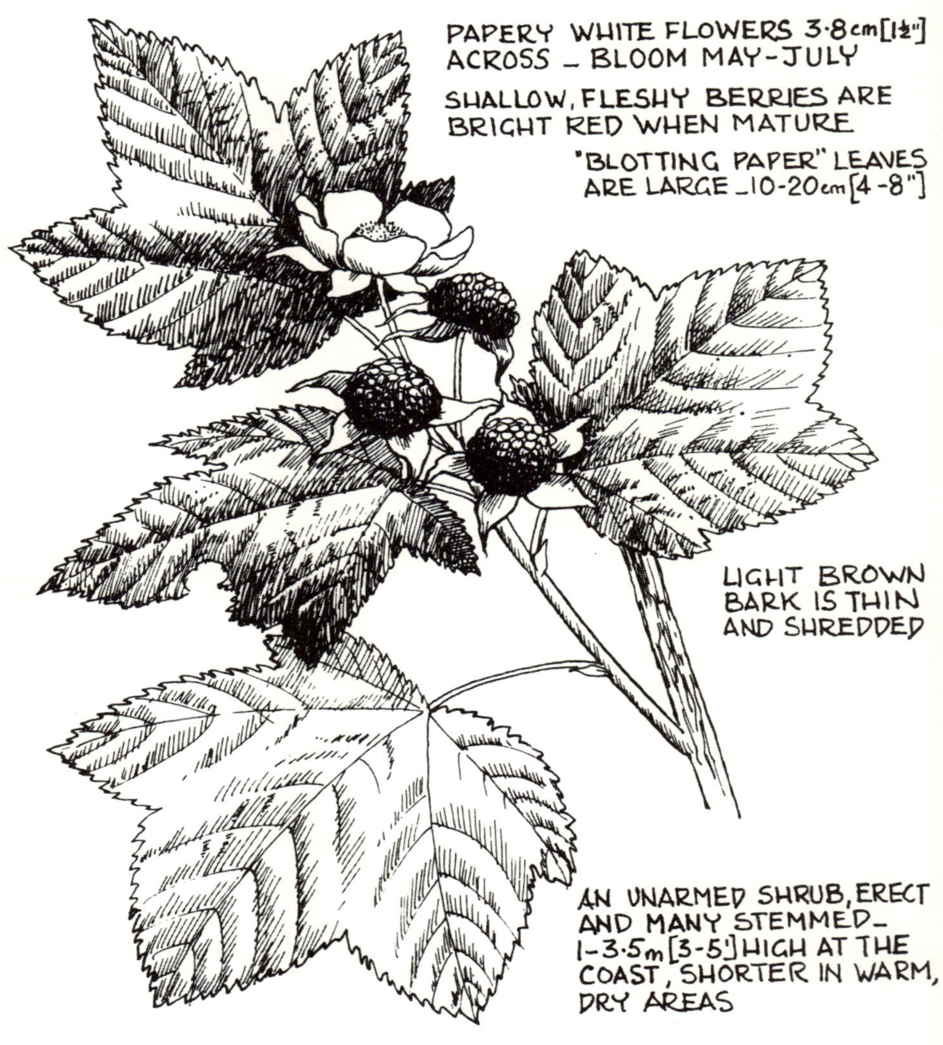

PAPERY WHITE FLOWERS 3·8cm[1½"]
ACROSS _ BLOOM MAY-JULY

SHALLOW, FLESHY BERRIES ARE
BRIGHT RED WHEN MATURE

"BLOTTING PAPER" LEAVES
ARE LARGE _10-20cm[4-8"]

LIGHT BROWN
BARK IS THIN
AND SHREDDED

AN UNARMED SHRUB, ERECT
AND MANY STEMMED_
1-3·5m[3-5'] HIGH AT THE
COAST, SHORTER IN WARM,
DRY AREAS

Thimbleberry

Rubus parviflorus

Habitat

Dense thickets of chest-high bushes grow in damp shady places along shorelines, forest edges, open clearings and roadsides, from southern British Columbia south to California. It also grows in dry interior regions, but not as tall.

Season

The leaves can be picked from spring through fall, but the old leaves of late fall make the best tea. The berries ripen in June and July.

Preparation

Pick large, soft leaves. Crush them and steep fresh, using a good handful per two-cup teapot. For extra flavour and colour, add a few crushed berries to the pot. To enjoy this tea in winter, dry both the leaves and the berries. Try mixing it with mint, sage, wintergreen or other herb teas.

Did you know...

First Nations peoples used the large leaves to lay food on and to cover baskets of food.

For a handy container to collect some of the berries, break off a really large leaf, stalk attached, and overlap the two sides to form a cone. Bend the stalk upwards and poke it like a pin through the overlapped edges of the leaves (see drawing). The leaves can also be used as a temporary lid for a jar, held on by a rubber band, or serve as a picnic plate for food. And because the leaves are soft and strong, they are a handy substitute for toilet paper out in the woods.

MOST VIOLET SPECIES HAVE
TOOTHED, HEART-SHAPED
LEAVES OF DARK GREEN

FLOWERS ARE ALL SIMILAR,
BUT COLOURS VARY FROM
WHITE TO PALE MAUVE, BLUE
AND YELLOW — BLOOMING
PERIOD SPANS APRIL TO JUNE

HEIGHT RANGES FROM LOW
TO THE GROUND, UP TO 25cm
[10"] TALL

Wild Violet

Viola adunca & other species

Habitat

Violets have a wide distribution from sea level to 1550 metres (5000 feet) and are easy to identify. They can be found enjoying sun or partial shade in woods and meadows, on hillsides and in many other places where conditions are favourable. Some species require more moisture than others.

Season

A few violets are evergreens and have leaves all year; others are spring-to-fall plants.

Preparation

Pick the leaves at any time of the year, remembering to spread your picking to minimize damage to the plants. Allow two teaspoons of crushed, dried leaves for each cup of boiling water and steep for 10 to 15 minutes. The garden variety of violet (if not sprayed with chemicals) also makes a good tea.

Did you know...

Wild violets do not have the fragrance of the cultivated species, but their leaves are high in vitamins A and C.

Crystallized violets are a charming decoration for cakes. The process is not difficult but requires care. Use only fresh, perfect flowers. Beat the white of an egg until slightly frothy. Gently holding a flower with tweezers, use an artist's small, soft-haired brush to coat every bit of it with the egg white, then dip it into finely granulated or berry sugar. Be sure to cover every part of the flower with egg white and sugar, or it will not preserve. Carefully place the flowers on waxed paper and leave in a warm place for 2 to 4 days until quite dry. You can also crystallize single rose petals or very small rose buds.

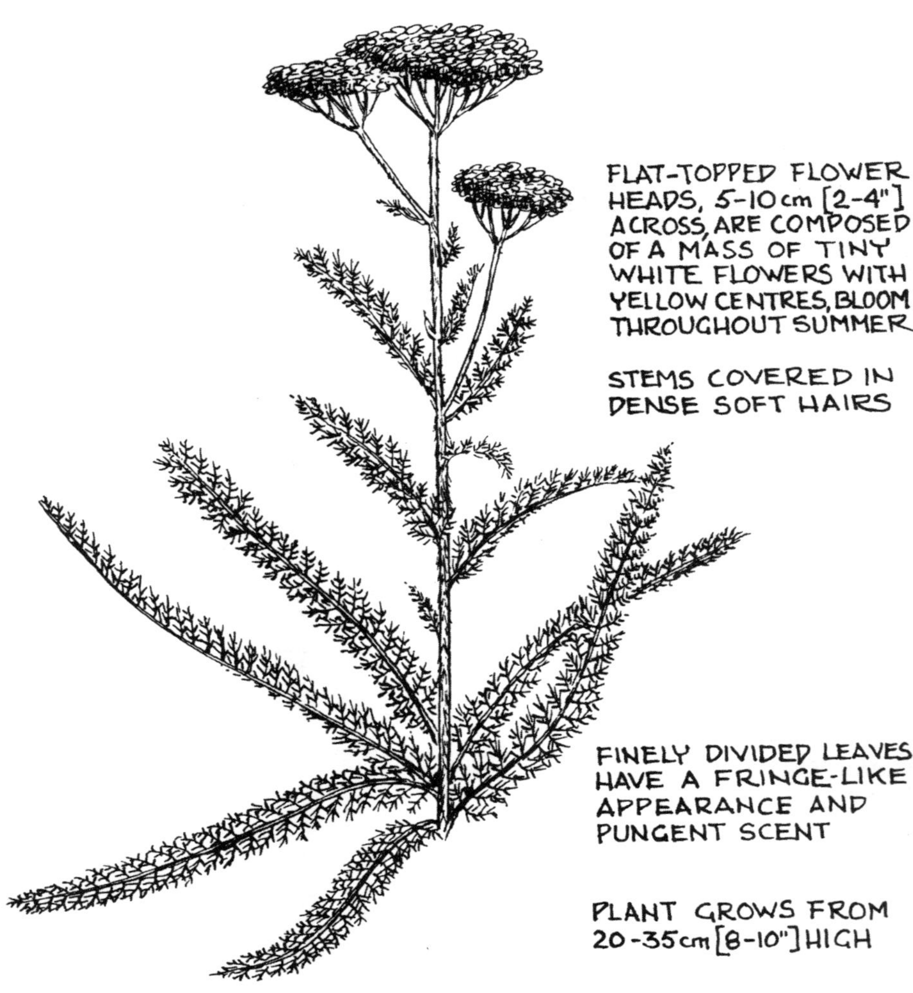

FLAT-TOPPED FLOWER
HEADS, 5-10 cm [2-4"]
ACROSS, ARE COMPOSED
OF A MASS OF TINY
WHITE FLOWERS WITH
YELLOW CENTRES, BLOOM
THROUGHOUT SUMMER

STEMS COVERED IN
DENSE SOFT HAIRS

FINELY DIVIDED LEAVES
HAVE A FRINGE-LIKE
APPEARANCE AND
PUNGENT SCENT

PLANT GROWS FROM
20-35cm [8-10"] HIGH

Yarrow

Achillea millefolium, Achillea lanulosa

Habitat

Where there is poor soil, where few other flowers will flourish, yarrow is there to brighten the scene with its showy, flat-topped flower heads. Look for it along roadsides and forest edges, on hillsides, and in vacant lots, dry meadows and other open areas.

Be careful not to confuse yarrow with another white flower—pearly everlasting—that often grows in a similar habitat.

Season

Yarrow flowers in its second year of growth. At any time during the summer and the fall, it can be used for tea.

Preparation

All parts of this strongly aromatic plant will make a beverage, but the leaves and flowers are the easiest to collect and dry. Many health food stores sell packaged dried yarrow flowers, whose curative powers have been known in Europe for hundreds of years.

To make a tea, steep one or two teaspoons of dried, crushed yarrow per cup of boiling water, then add honey to taste.

Did you know...

The straight, dried stalks of yarrow are used by many people to throw the *I Ching*. The Haida enjoyed the flavour of butter clams that had been strung on yarrow stalks to dry, and people of the Okanagan First Nation made an insect deterrent by burning yarrow leaves on hot embers.

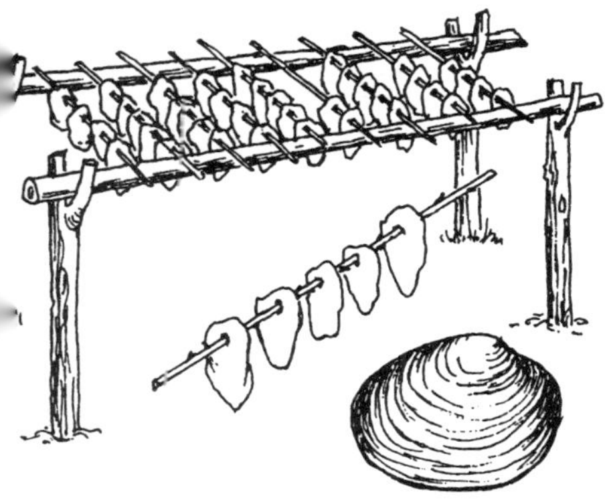

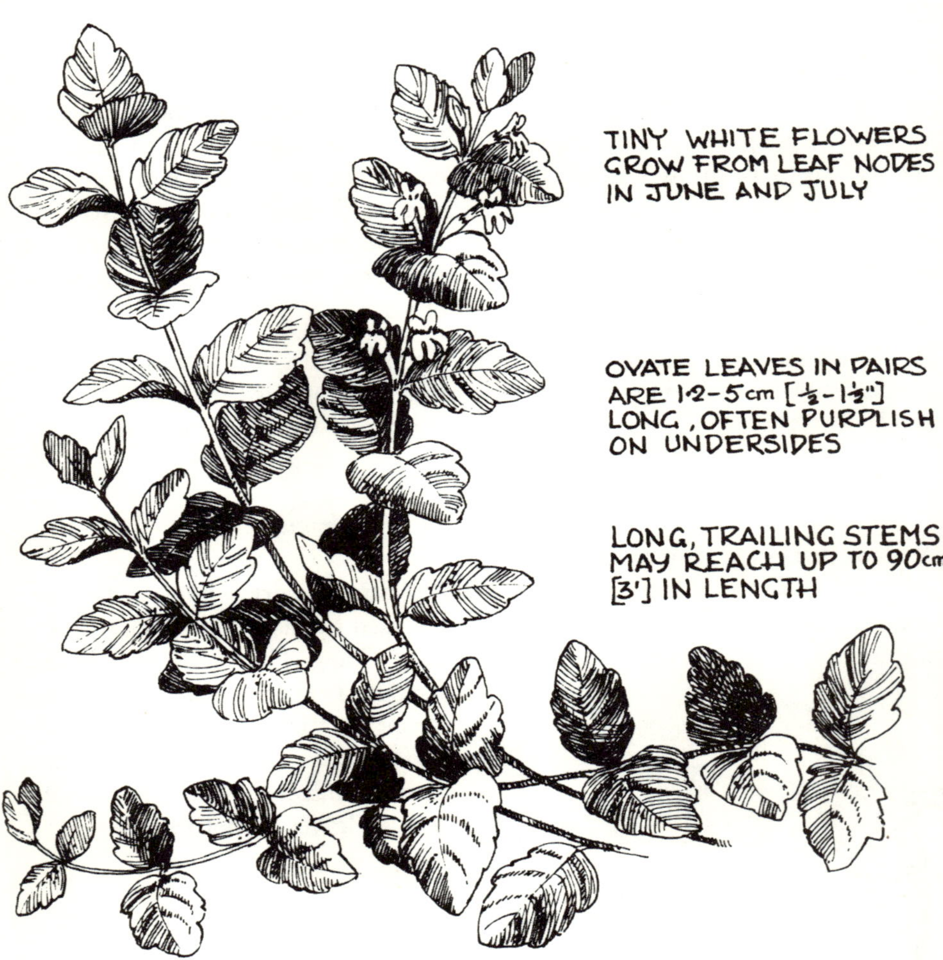

TINY WHITE FLOWERS
GROW FROM LEAF NODES
IN JUNE AND JULY

OVATE LEAVES IN PAIRS
ARE 1·2-5cm [½-1½"]
LONG, OFTEN PURPLISH
ON UNDERSIDES

LONG, TRAILING STEMS
MAY REACH UP TO 90cm
[3'] IN LENGTH

Yerba Buena

Satureja douglasii

Other Name

Oregon Tea

Habitat

This trailing member of the mint family spreads across the ground of open coniferous woods, dry fields and slopes. It favours southwestern British Columbia on through Washington and Oregon to California.

Season

The woody rhizome of yerba buena puts out new growth in the spring and early summer. Look for this herb throughout the summer months when it is most abundant. You may also find it in the fall in warm, sheltered areas.

Preparation

Pick a small handful of these wonderfully scented leaves, crush and steep in a cupful of boiling water to make a remarkably good tea. As with other members of the mint family, the leaves are best used fresh, but they can also be dried if desired.

Did you know...

The enchanting name yerba buena, meaning good herb, comes to us through the early Spanish priests of California who long ago recognized the healthful virtues of the plant.

Making Jam and Jelly

Preliminaries

I am going to assume that readers who want to make the
jam and jelly recipes that follow already have some knowledge
of this category of cooking. There are many fine points in jam
and jelly making; these relate to utensils, fruit combinations,
quantities, pectin (powdered, liquid or none), acidity, boiling
times, temperature, testing, sterilizing jars, sealing, and so on.
Inexperienced preserve makers may wish to refer to a book on
this subject for all the details.

Here, I give recipes for making simple jams and jellies, and
an easy method of using melted wax to seal re-used jars, as
opposed to using a costly box of a dozen canning jars with
two-piece lids.

Because most wild fruits have more juice than pulp, jelly is
often a more appropriate use than jam. However, other fruits,
such as apple, pineapple, plum, etc. can be added to create jams
with interesting flavours.

Equipment Required

The items needed to make simple jams and jellies are few and
readily available:

- Two saucepans. One for cooking the jam or jelly, preferably
  with a heavy base that fits the cooking surface (you will not
  need a lid, as the excess moisture must evaporate). Another
  (preferably an old one, or a double boiler) for melting the
  paraffin wax.
- A potato masher for crushing fruit.
- A long-handled wooden spoon for stirring and testing for the
  jelly stage.
- A jelly bag, which can be bought or made from several layers
  of cheesecloth. A friend of mine cuts off a big corner of an old
  pillowcase, allowing ample room to hold the fruit.

- Glass jars of various sizes. Commercially sold canning jars, medium and small, complete with lids, often have a design of fruits molded into the glass. Classy, but I'd rather use recycled jars. I prefer to use small jars for jam and jelly, rather than large ones. For one thing, many wild fruits cannot be gathered in quantity. Also, that way I have more to give away to friends; and besides, they look so good all lined up on a shelf.
- A measuring cup.
- A packet of paraffin wax (as used for candle-making or waxing skis).
- Some clean, thick string.
- Stick-on labels (store-bought or make your own) to identify the contents and date.

Preparation

Once you're back in your kitchen, spread out all the fruit on a shallow tray and pick through it, discarding bits of leaves and stems, any rotten fruit or even hitchhiking critters. Place the fruit in a sieve or colander and rinse well with cold water.

Sterilizing Glass Jars

Wash the jars in hot soapy water and rinse well. Immerse the jars in a pot of hot water and bring to a boil. Boil for 15 to 20 minutes, then remove the jars and turn them upside down on a clean surface to drain and dry. Fill them with jam or jelly as soon as possible when they're dry but still hot.

Testing for the Jelly Stage

If you are making jelly, test to see if it's reached the right stage by dipping a wooden spoon into the boiling liquid and lifting it out. The jelly stage is approaching when two drops fall from the spoon's edge. Continue testing from time to time until the two drops run together and slide off in a sheet—a sign that the jelling process is complete.

Filling and Sealing Jars

When the jam or jelly is ready, skim off any foam. For jelly, use a measuring cup to transfer the hot liquid from the pan to the jar. For jam, use a large spoon. The sterilized jars should be dry and hot when you fill them. Use a damp cloth to wipe off any particles on the glass in order to insure a good seal.

To melt the wax, place one block (broken into a few pieces to speed the process) in an old saucepan or double boiler. When the jam or jelly in the jars is no longer steaming, pour a little hot wax over the entire surface to a thickness of 3 mm (1/8"). When cool, add a second layer of wax, rotating the jar to form a total seal.

Here's a handy tip. Place a 10-cm (4-inch) length of thick string across the first layer of hot wax, with one end hanging well over the edge of the jar. Once the first layer sets, pour in more wax to the top of the jar, rotating as you do, to insure a perfect seal. (When it's time to remove the wax seal so that you can spoon out the jam, simply pull up the string to lift out the wax all in one piece.)

Labelling and Storing

Don't forget to label jars with the contents and date. It's frustrating to bring out a jar of reddish jelly and not remember what fruit you made it from. You can buy fancy labels or make your own, perhaps adding a colourful illustration of the berry used. If you wish, you may photocopy a part of the illustration in this book (reducing it as necessary) and colour it.

For a final decorative touch, cut a circle of any suitable fabric you may have, preferably using pinking shears. Place this over the jar and secure it with a rubber band. You can cover the rubber band with a ribbon and a bow.

Store the jars in a cool, dry place. If perfectly sealed, the contents will last a year or two, maybe longer. I don't know exactly, as mine get eaten up or given away. Should you find a spot of mould in the jar, just spoon it out and throw away; the rest will be perfectly edible.

Always refrigerate after opening.

Jam and Jelly Recipes

Quick Blackberry Jam

For an interesting variation, add some crushed salal berries (about 25 per cent should be salal).

6 cups	fully ripe blackberries	1.5 L
	sugar	

Place the berries in a saucepan and crush with a potato masher. Bring to a full rolling boil for 3 minutes. Measure the quantity of pulp and add an equal amount of sugar warmed in the oven.

Reheat the berries and maintain a full rolling boil for 3 minutes. Remove the pot from the stove and stir the pulp with an eggbeater for another 3 minutes. (To avoid getting splashed with hot pulp, poke the eggbeater through a hole or slit in a sheet of heavy paper or card that is large enough to cover the saucepan.) Skim off any foam. Spoon into hot sterilized jars and seal.

Spiced Crab Apple Jelly

4 lbs.	crab apples	2 kg
	water to cover	
	juice of lemon(s)	
	powdered cinnamon	
	sugar	

Cut up the crab apples and place in a saucepan, then add water to cover. Cook for 30 minutes, crushing with a potato masher and stirring occasionally. Strain the pulp through a jelly bag, pressing out all the juice.

Measure the juice. For each cup (250 mL) of liquid, add 1 tablespoon (15 mL) of lemon juice and 1/16 teaspoon (0.25 mL) of cinnamon. Pour into a saucepan and bring to a boil. Add 2/3 cup (175 mL) of warm sugar for each cup (250 mL) of liquid. Boil rapidly without stirring, except to test for the jelly stage. Skim off any foam. Pour into hot sterilized jars and seal.

Huckleberry Jam

4 cups	ripe huckleberries	1 L
2 Tbsp.	lemon juice	30 mL
1/4 tsp.	salt	1 mL
3 cups	sugar	750 mL

Place all the ingredients together in a saucepan. Bring to a boil, stirring frequently, until thick. Skim off any foam. As this jam sets quickly, spoon immediately into hot sterilized jars and seal.

Mountain Ash Jelly

For a different flavour, add a large sprig of mint before boiling to the jelly stage. Remove and discard the mint before pouring the jelly into jars.

fully ripe mountain ash berries
water
sugar

Place the berries in a saucepan and just cover with cold water. Boil until the berries are soft and crush with a potato masher. Strain the pulp through a jelly bag, pressing out all the juice.

Measure the juice, then boil for 25 minutes. Gradually add 1 cup (250 mL) sugar for each cup (250 mL) of juice, stirring all the while. Boil to the jelly stage, about 10 minutes. Skim off any foam. Pour into hot sterilized jars and seal.

Oregon Grape Jelly

>fully ripe Oregon grapes
>cold water
>sugar

Place the grapes in a saucepan and barely cover with water. Simmer gently until tender, then crush with a potato masher. Strain the pulp through a jelly bag, pressing out all the juice.

Measure the juice, then place in a saucepan and bring to a boil for 5 minutes. (NOTE: Use only 3 to 4 cups / 750 mL to 1 L of juice at a time.) Add an equal amount of sugar and bring to a boil until it reaches the jelly stage. Skim off any foam. Pour into hot sterilized jars and seal.

Salal Berry Jam

This is one of my favourite jams, maybe because I am surrounded by salal bushes but also because it is so simple to make and the flavour is really delicious. Many people just make a jelly from the berries, but why throw away all that tasty pulp? (Note that eating a quantity of this jam can slightly stain your teeth and tongue—but not for long, and the flavour is worth it.)

6 cups	fully ripe salal berries	1.5 L
1/2 cup	water	125 mL
1 1/2 cups	sugar	325 mL
1 tsp.	vanilla or almond extract	5 mL

Place the berries and water in a saucepan on medium heat, stirring and crushing with a potato masher. Gradually add the sugar, all the while stirring and mashing until no berries remain whole. Bring to a boil and continue stirring for 20 minutes.

Check for sweetness and add more sugar if required. Stir in the vanilla or almond extract. Skim off any foam. Spoon into hot sterilized jars and seal.

Salal Berry Jelly

To cut the strong natural taste and give an interesting flavour to this jelly, add 1 cup (250 mL) of canned crushed pineapple to each cup (250 mL) of juice.

> salal berries
> cold water
> vanilla or almond extract
> sugar

Place the salal berries in a saucepan and add water to cover. Cook for 12 minutes, crushing with a potato masher.

Strain the pulp through a jelly bag, pressing out all the juice.

Measure the resulting juice and add an equal amount of sugar. Pour the juice into a saucepan and cook until it reaches the jelly stage. Stir in the vanilla or almond extract to taste. Skim off any foam. Pour into hot sterilized jars and seal.

Wild Strawberry Jam

Wild strawberries have a flavour that is far superior to those that are commercially grown. They take a lot of picking because of their small size, but they are worth it.

4 cups	crushed strawberries	1 L
1 1/2 Tbsp.	vinegar	20 mL
4 cups	sugar	1 L

Combine the crushed strawberries and vinegar in a saucepan and bring to a full rolling boil for 3 minutes. Add the sugar, stirring constantly, and return to a full boil for another 6 minutes. Skim off any foam. Spoon into hot sterilized jars and seal.

Select Bibliography

Benoliel, Doug. *Northwest Foraging*. Signpost Publishing, Edmonds, Wash. 1974.

Bergland, Berndt, & Clare E. Polsby. *The Edible Wild*. Pagurian Press, Toronto. 1971.

Clark, Lewis J. *Wild Flowers of the Pacific Northwest*. Gray's Publishing, Sidney, B.C. 1976.

Frankton, Clarence, & Gerald A. Mulligan. *Weeds of Canada*. Dept. of Agriculture, Ottawa. 1970.

Gilkey, Helen M. *Handbook of Northwest Coast Flowering Plants*. Binfords & Mort, Portland, Oregon. 1961.

Gunther, Erna. *Ethnobotany of Western Washington*. University of Washington Press, Seattle. 1973.

Haskin, Leslie L. *Wild Flowers of the Pacific Coast*. Binfords & Mort, Portland, Oregon. 1934.

Hitchcock, Leo, et al. *Vascular Plants of the Pacific Northwest*. 5 vols. University of Washington Press, Seattle. 1955–69.

Scully, Virginia. *A Treasury of American Herbs*. Bonanza Books, New York. 1970.

Turner, Nancy J. *Food Plants of the British Columbia Indians, Part 1: Coastal Peoples*. British Columbia Provincial Museum, Victoria. 1975.

——. *Food Plants of the British Columbia Indians, Part 2: Interior Peoples*. British Columbia Provincial Museum, Victoria. 1975.

——. *Plants in British Columbia Indian Technology*. British Columbia Provincial Museum, Victoria. 1979.

—— & Adam F. Szczawinski. *Wild Coffee and Tea Substitutes of Canada*. National Museums of Canada, Ottawa. 1978.

The Plants and Their Uses

TEAS

Bee balm
Biscuitroot
Blackcap
Blackberry
Blue sailors
Chickweed
Clover
Douglas-fir
Fireweed
Wild ginger
Goldenrod
Ground ivy
Gumweed
Western hemlock
Huckleberry
Juniper
Kinnikinnick
Labrador tea
Western larch
Wild mint
Nettle
Pine
Pineapple weed
Rose
Sagebrush
Sheep sorrel
Snowbrush
Stink currant
Wild strawberry
Thimbleberry
Wild violet
Yarrow
Yerba buena

COFFEES

Bedstraw
Scotch broom
Blue sailors
Dandelion

LEMONADES

Buffaloberry
Mountain Ash
Mountain sorrel
Sheep sorrel
Sumac

CORDIALS

Blackberry
Pacific crab apple
Huckleberry
Oregon grape
Salal
Salmonberry
Wild strawberry

OTHER DRINKS

Blackcap
Kinnikinnick
Hairy manzanita
Pipsissewa
Salmonberry
Wild sarsaparilla
Self-heal
Sweet gale

JAMS AND JELLIES

Blackberry
Pacific crab apple
Huckleberry
Mountain ash
Oregon grape
Salal
Wild strawberry

Notes